# HOW TO WRITE F

**In this Series**

*other titles in preparation*

# WRITE FOR PUBLICATION

Chriss McCallum

**Northcote House**

First published in 1989 by Northcote House Publishers Ltd, Harper & Row House, Estover Road, Plymouth PL6 7PZ, United Kingdom. Tel: Plymouth (0752) 705251. Telex: 45635. Fax: (0752) 777603.

**British Library Cataloguing in Publication Data**

McCallum, Chriss, *1935–*
   How to write for publication.—(How to books).
   1. Authorship – Manuals
   I. Title II. Series
   808′.02

   ISBN 0-7463-0538-9

*Printed and bound in Great Britain by A. Wheaton & Co., Ltd., Exeter*

# Contents

# Preface

You want to write, and you want to get your writing published. Where do you start?

**You need to know:**
- What to write.
- How to write it.
- Where to sell it.

**You need a guide**

It's a bit of a maze, this writing business. You'll be surprised how big it is, too. It's no use wandering about on your own. You'll only waste time and effort — and money.

Try to resist the itch to pick up a pen till you've taken the round trip. You'll be ready then to decide which point of entry you want to try first.

Hold on to the string...

**Acknowledgements**

For permission to publish original quotes, copyright material and personal experiences, the author and publishers thank Alan Bond, Patricia Brennan, John Brown, Wally K. Daly, Richard Drew, J. T. Edson, Peter Finch, Robert Goddard, Robbie Gray, Diann Greenhow, Richard Halford, Paul Heapy, Joan B. Howes, Ted Hughes, Philip Hutton-Wilson, Lewis Jones, H. R. F. Keating, Joyce Lister, Brian Lumley, Dorothy Lumley, Diana Mills, Harry Mulholland, Mike Pattinson, Peggy Poole, Ken Rock, Pat Saunders, Jean Sergeant, Liz Taylor, Graham Thomas, D. C. Thomson & Co. Ltd, Gordon Wells, Steve Wetton and Charles R. Wickins.

**Author's Note**

Editors and publishers, like writers, spring from both sexes. If anyone can invent a workable device to convey that fact neatly and without the awkward use of 'he and she', 'he/she', '(s)he' and suchlike, I'll be glad if you'll send it on. In the meantime, please read 'he', 'him' and 'his' throughout the text as embracing both men and women. No sexism is intended — after all, despite my slightly androgynous name, I am a woman.

# 1
# Getting Started

**BEFORE YOU STEP IN**

To be a writer, all you have to do is apply your pen to paper, and let the words flow out. Writing for the sheer pleasure of expressing your thoughts and feelings is a very satisfying activity.

But it isn't satisfying enough for *you*, is it? You don't just want to be a writer — you want to be a *published* writer.

There are no foolproof methods. There are no absolute rules. You can write anything you like. To get your work into print, however, there's one fact of life you can't afford to ignore: writing for publication is a hard-headed and fiercely competitive business. If you accept that at the outset, you'll approach your writing and the business of selling it in the best way and with the best chance of success.

It's a buyer's market. Don't underestimate what that means. The acceptance rate for unsolicited book manuscripts, for instance, is about one in two thousand — very long odds. But you *can* shorten them. You can:

- Get to know how the publishing business works.
- Learn how to identify, analyse and approach your markets.
- Understand why you have to offer editors what they want, not what you think they *should* want.
- Learn how to develop a mutually profitable *professional* relationship with the editors you want to do business with.

The writing world is full of hopeful authors who will never see a word of theirs in print, because they don't — or won't — understand that they have to study and work at both the craft of writing and the art of selling.

**First serve your apprenticeship**

There's no secret recipe, no magic formula for success. Tedious it might sound, but the only way to succeed is to *work*. Writing is a creative art, yes, but the art can only be developed from a sound knowledge of the craft. You would never dream, would you, of getting up on a public platform to play the piano if you didn't know one note from another? Yet legions of writers bombard editorial offices with manuscripts that are unstructured, badly written and all-too-often directed to the wrong publisher anyway. These writers are constantly amazed and upset because their manuscripts boomerang home trailing rejection slips.

You don't have to court such disappointment. You can take the time and trouble to learn:

● the **basic techniques** of good writing;
● how to **structure** your writing;
● how to **choose and use** language to the best possible effect;
● how to **communicate your thoughts** without muddle or ambiguity;
● how to **capture and hold your reader's interest**;
● how to **revise and rewrite**, and rewrite again till you're sure the work is as good as you can make it.

Throughout this book you'll find references to books and magazines, courses, associations, services and information sources that will help you to master the craft of writing and develop the skills you need to succeed in getting your work published. To avoid unnecessary repetition, you'll find the full details in the appendices — names, addresses, telephone numbers, and prices and subscription/membership rates where applicable.

You'll also read words of wisdom, encouragement and occasionally caution, from editors and from published writers, some of whom are just at the beginning of their career but many of whom are well established and well known. You don't have to agree with them — they don't always agree with each other — but what they have to say is well worth reading. These are people who know the business. They want to help *you* to know it too.

**Take yourself seriously**

It isn't easy to think of yourself as a serious writer when you're just starting out. You're probably worried about your chances of success, and nagged by doubts that wake you up in the small hours. Maybe you're worried because you can't make up your mind about what kind of writing is right for you. Don't worry. Most writers feel like this at first — and those who are *too* sure of themselves tend to trip over their own egos. Have confidence in your own capacity to learn. Approach your writing *from the beginning* in a professional manner. After all, if you don't believe in your potential ability, how can you expect to convince others?

> As I myself found, one of the biggest deterrents at the beginning of a writing career is the inability to take yourself seriously. It seems as if you are yearning after an impossible dream, seeking to enter a world inhabited by the greats. It is difficult to realise that most other writers have started with the same doubts and uncertainties.
>
> Liz Taylor, *The Writing Business*.

## And be taken seriously

The first part of the book is designed to help you build your credibility. It will give you a working knowledge of the business of writing and its accepted practices and conventions, so that you can avoid many of the pitfalls that commonly beset the inexperienced writer.

This knowledge will also equip you to decide more easily where you want to start, and you'll get far more out of the information in the second part. Even if you've already chosen your field (or if your field has chosen you, as often happens), don't disregard the other options altogether. You might want to branch out later on.

## Common sense

Many beginner writers seem to be drawn to one or the other of two extreme attitudes. First, there's the new writer who devours all the advice he can lay hands on, and who treats every word as gospel. He then gets himself into a terrible twist, endlessly trying to adapt his style, his approach, his technique, his marketing strategy, because the writers' magazine or manual he's reading this week contradicts the advice in the one he read last week. He has no faith at all in his own judgement, and gives himself no chance to develop any.

Then there's the opposite type, the beginner who refuses to consider *any* advice or help from anyone. He drives editors to distraction by disregarding even the most basic common-sense principles. He's the one who shoots off book-length stories to tiny magazines, single poems to book publishers, erudite essays to mass-market magazines...

Neither of these writers uses his common sense. The result is that they create problems where none existed before.

This book aims to show you the practical common-sense ways to succeed in getting your work published. Above all, it will enable you to develop reliance on your own judgement, based on the information you'll read here and in the recommended books, and then on the experience you'll gradually acquire for yourself.

Here, then, are a few basic common-sense DOs and DON'Ts to bear in mind as you read:

1. DO study the techniques of good, clear writing, but DON'T submerge your individual instincts.
2. DO study your markets to make sure the material you send them is suitable, but DON'T carbon-copy the style and content so closely that you sacrifice every trace of originality.
3. DO be courteous and businesslike in all your dealings with editors, but DON'T regard them either as enemies or as gods. They're not 'anti' new writers, or unapproachable, or infallible, or exalted — they're human beings with problems and prejudices, mortgages and falling hair, just like the rest of us.
4. DO work at cultivating your own judgement, but DON'T attempt to defy the conventions before you understand them.
5. And, above all, DO write. DON'T just think or talk or read or dream about writing. *Do it*.

## HOW TO GET STARTED

In theory, all you need is a pen and a pad of paper. In practice, it isn't that simple. Editors won't read handwritten scripts. You need to be able to present your work in the form of a typescript. Though it looks like a contradiction in terms, this is usually called a **manuscript** (abbreviation 'ms', plural 'mss').

You'll save a lot of money if you can type your ms yourself. A professional typist charges upwards of £3 per 1,000 words plus extra for copies (and you need at least one complete copy). A 60,000 word novel, then, could cost about £200 just for typing, more than the price of a new portable. Even two or three short stories would cost you at least £8 to £10.

It isn't difficult to learn. There are evening classes, or you could teach yourself quite quickly with a simple manual like Brenda Rowe's *Type It Yourself*.

## BASIC EQUIPMENT

You need pens, and small notebooks you can carry in your pocket or bag, to note *anything* that might be useful. Ideas, words, phrases, overheard anecdotes can slip away forever if you don't get them down on paper at the time. Students' A4 lined notepads are popular with writers who write their first drafts in longhand. Others prefer to work straight on to a typewriter or word processor. Whichever method you choose, you'll eventually need the following to market your writing:

- If you work on a word processor, a decent letter-quality printer. Most editors dislike dot-matrix printers — some even refuse to read work produced on them.
- For typewritten mss, plain white A4 bond paper, for top copies. (Don't waste it on notes or drafts — anything will do for those. Save unwanted flyers, defunct letters and the like.)
- A4 bank paper, for carbon copies. Use coloured bank for your own file copies if you like, but don't send out coloured sheets.
- Black A4 carbon paper.
- Black typewriter ribbons. Don't economise on these — replace them *before* they wear out.
- Plain white business envelopes, 9″ x 4½″.
- 'Giant' manilla envelopes, 9″ x 6½″, to hold A4 sheets folded once.

Office supply shops are cheaper than high street stationers for paper and envelopes. Shop around and compare prices. If you're a reasonably good typist, you could use A4 plain copier paper (it doesn't erase well). Ask for 80 gsm (grammes per square metre) weight. It's about half the price of bond. Make friends with your local office supplier. He might give you a small discount if you buy all your stationery supplies there.

### Do you need a word processor?
No, you don't. If you have one already, then of course you'll use it, but if you don't, then don't rush out and buy one on the strength of anticipated earnings from your writing. A word processor is a sophisticated tool, but it isn't a writer. Remember the computing term GIGO — Garbage In, Garbage Out. Nothing and no one can do the creating but you.

Every successful writer works in his or her own way. Russell Hoban said during a Writers-on-Tour seminar that it took him four years to master his Apple II, but now he would never work any other way. (He even gave his Apple a starring role in his novel *The Medusa Frequency*.) But Fay Weldon, interviewed on Channel Four, declared that if the day ever comes when she's required to write on a machine, she'll stop writing. She writes with a pen and pad, and pays someone else to type her mss.

**For word processor/computer enthusiasts**
There's a bi-monthly magazine, *The Wordsmith*, for writers who work on computers. It's particularly helpful if you're interested in self-publishing, community publishing and so on.

A recent book you might find useful, too, is *The Writer and the Word Processor* by Ray Hammond.

## USEFUL BOOKS

Buy these books if you can — you'll use them a lot:

- A big fat dictionary — *Chambers 20th Century* is a good one.
- An up-to-date copy of the *Writers' & Artists' Yearbook*, a directory of book and magazine publishers, with names, addresses, telephone numbers and information about what they publish. It also gives sound advice about writing and publishing, agents, associations, services, taxation liabilities, rights, copyright and so on.
- *The Oxford Dictionary for Writers and Editors*, very useful for checking difficult spellings and usage, including lots of proper names, capitalisation, abbreviations, foreign words and phrases.
- *Research for Writers* by Ann Hoffmann, the best reference book for finding information sources.
- A concise encyclopedia, like the annual *Pears Cyclopedia*.
- *Roget's Thesaurus*, lists synonyms for almost every word in the English language. Marvellous for finding just the right word — but don't get addicted.
- *The Writer's Handbook*, a new writers' directory which appeared for the first time in 1988. The first serious rival to the *Writers' & Artists' Yearbook*, it doesn't list as many publishers as the *Yearbook* but gives much more detailed information about those it does include, and covers more radio, TV and stage outlets. Use it as a complement to the *Yearbook* rather than a substitute.

**Books about writing**
There are dozens of books to show you how to write publishable work. You'll find details of books about writing for specific fields in the appropriate sections later in the book. The books listed below are recommended especially for new writers who want to familiarise themselves with the practice and business of writing.

- *An Author's Guide to Publishing* by Michael Legat. Lots of information about book publishing, contracts, presentation, author–publisher relations.
- *Writing for Pleasure and Profit* by Michael Legat. Very readable

coverage of many fields of writing, and particularly good on novels.

- *The Writing Business* by Liz Taylor. Enthusiastic, encouraging and practical — rich in insights into the writer's world and work.
- *The Way to Write* by John Fairfax and John Moat. The originators of the Arvon Foundation explain the basic techniques of good writing.

## FINDING WHAT YOU NEED

### Library services

The public library should be able to get *any* book that's in print for you, and many that are out of print, from other libraries or from the inter-library loan service which operates through the British Lending Library. Depending on how difficult it is to get the book you want, there might be a small charge if the inter-library loan service is used. Your library will advise you.

As you'll probably be using the library a good deal, it's worth making a note of the main category divisions of the Dewey Decimal Classification System, which is used in most UK libraries. The category numbers are shown on the shelves, and it saves time if you know where to start looking:

| | | | |
|---|---|---|---|
| 000 | General Works | 500 | Science |
| 100 | Philosophy | 600 | Technology |
| 200 | Religion | 700 | The Arts and Recreations |
| 300 | Social Sciences | 800 | Literature |
| 400 | Languages | 900 | Geography, Biography and History |

### Out of print books and books on your special subjects

The monthly *Book and Magazine Collector* lists books for sale and wanted. Although it's primarily intended for book dealers and collectors, it's useful for writers, too. Many dealers specialise, and you can ask them to put you on their mailing lists. Or you can advertise for books yourself.

### Bookfinding service

Jubilee Books is run by Geoff and Karinda FitzGerald, who specialise in finding all kinds of books from all over the world. Their booksearch service is free of charge, without obligation, and all books are sent to customers post free. You only pay for the book or books found for you.

You should provide as much information about the book as possible — title, author, date of publication if you know it, and state whether or not you want a first edition. This service also handles comics, annuals and all printed ephemera.

## Writers' magazines

There are a few magazines specially produced for writers. They print advice, news, reviews, competition notices and other information on what's happening on the writing scene, plus articles by writers discussing the craft and business of writing.

The longest established is *Success*, which is particularly useful to the beginning writer. It's a service magazine, not a glossy, and it's packed with information. There's a Manuscript Folio System, a kind of postal workshop. Each folio has up to eight members, who comment, criticise and advise on each other's work, under the guidance of an editor who is also a published writer. There are folios for many different types of writing, including articles, short stories, novels, writing for children, poetry and so on. Membership of a folio (which is entirely optional) is included in the magazine subscription. *Success* is published every two months.

*Writing* is a small privately published magazine, with articles about writers and writing, news, views and reviews of books about writing. *Writing* also publishes a few poems and short stories contributed by its readers.

*The Writers' Rostrum* and *Writers' Own Magazine* are two more publications similar in content to *Writing*, and very encouraging to new writers.

*Writer's Monthly* is a glossy A4 magazine, very professional-looking, full of information and discussion about writers and writing, with many well known names as contributors.

*Freelance Writing and Photography* is a long-established writers' magazine. It was taken into new ownership in 1987, and has been undergoing a series of changes, including its format. At the time of writing, its future style and content are not yet clear, but by the time you read this, it should have settled down under its new editor. It was always a reliable publication, and it's worth having a look at it to see what it has to offer you.

*The Author* and *The Writers' Newsletter* are, respectively, the official magazines of The Society of Authors and The Writers' Guild of Great Britain. Non-members can buy them on subscription.

## Press cuttings service

Mrs Pat Kenderdine runs a press cuttings service for writers. You can borrow a batch of press cuttings and/or arrange for cuttings to be gathered for you on your own subject. A month's loan of a batch of cuttings costs from £1.50, depending on the number and value of the cuttings. Mrs Kenderdine doesn't issue lists, but deals with each enquiry on an individual basis, according to the writer's needs.

## Finding photographs

If you need photographs to illustrate your book, you'll find a list of photographic agencies and picture libraries in the *Writers' & Artists' Yearbook*. One of the largest agencies is Popperfoto (Paul Popper Limited), whose commercially available visual material amounts to a staggering 15,000,000 illustrations. Popperfoto lend their material worldwide, usually on a same-day basis, for reproduction purposes. It's mainly publishers who use these services, but a private individual can use them, too. However, the cost is quite high, a service fee of £12 payable whether or not you use the illustrations, and charges ranging from £27 for one black and white photograph with UK rights only, to £130 for a whole page colour photograph with all world and language rights. These are similar to most agencies' fees.

Mrs Liz Moore, manager of Popperfoto, always advises authors:

● not to start researching pictures till you have a publisher;
● wherever possible leave the research to the publisher — they know far more about it than authors;
● make sure you have it in writing that the publisher will be responsible for payments and for the safekeeping of the photos, otherwise *you* might be charged for any damage.

There's an excellent book on the subject, *The Art of Picture Research* by Hilary Evans. You can buy the book through booksellers or direct from Mr Evans. *See* under **Books for Writers**, page 172.

### Your local photographic society

There are probably quite a few members of your local photographic society who would be delighted to supply you with photographs. You could come to an arrangement about making payment if and when your material is published, and give an undertaking that the photographer's work will be credited to him.

### Free photographs

Many of our large industrial and commercial companies will allow you to use photographs of their products and related items free of charge, provided you give the company due acknowledgement and therefore publicity.

If there's a company whose products and/or services might be suitable as illustrations for your book or article, it's worth contacting their publicity officer to enquire about this.

You could also try enquiring at tourist information centres. Some of these will supply free slides or prints to accompany material that promotes their area.

## INSPIRATION, SUPPORT AND TUITION

Writing can be a lonely business. Some writers prefer to work alone, but others need the stimulation of company, to spark off ideas and exchange thoughts and views (and complaints about editors and agents). Once you start looking for kindred spirits, you'll be surprised how many there are around you.

### Writers' groups
There might be a writers' group already meeting in your district, or at least close enough for you to attend occasionally. Your library will have contact names and addresses.

*'Is this where they write Spitting Image, Engelbert?'*

You can get a *Directory of Writers' Circles*, compiled by Jill Dick, which lists contact names and addresses throughout the UK. Details are in the appendices, under **Useful Booklets**.

If there isn't a group near you, think about starting one yourself. A notice in your local paper (contact the editor) or pinned up in the library could turn up at least one or two fellow scribes. You can meet once or twice a month in each other's homes, or just meet occasionally but keep in touch by telephone. With enough members, you could hire a room regularly and share the cost.

Meeting other writers in a group can help in several ways. A group is mutually supportive, providing encouragement and comfort. As well as discussing work and problems, you can share the cost of subscriptions to writers' magazines, and build up a library of writers' manuals and reference books. Each member can contribute magazines to a market study collection, and you could club together to buy stationery in bulk.

Your local Arts Council Office will advise you about inviting guest speakers, and will help you to find them.

**Classes, seminars and residential courses**
Most **Local Education Authority (LEA)** and **Workers' Educational Association (WEA) courses** include some on creative writing and related subjects. These are usually advertised in the local press before the start of each term, and your library should have information.

**Seminars** and **courses** are held all over the country and all through the year. As you become familiar with the writer's world, and begin to receive the information that comes in and with writers' magazines, you'll find a surprising number of events you can take part in.

Writers who get involved in seminars and residential courses find that their enthusiasm and enjoyment carries over into writing at home, and keeps them going when they might otherwise become discouraged. This inspiration and encouragement is evident to the tutors as well as their students. Ted Hughes, the Poet Laureate, takes an active part in the Arvon Foundation, and is enthusiastic in his support of the courses:

---

On a good course, the excitement and delight of the students has to be seen to be believed. And no-one would credit the transformation it works on many of them, unless he had seen it. The whole course is designed to achieve this result, and nine times out of ten it does achieve it. The tutors want it to happen, and the students want it to happen, so it happens.

Ted Hughes, the Poet Laureate.

---

The **Arvon Foundation** offers residential courses at its two centres, Lumb Bank in Yorkshire and Totleigh Barton in Devon. Five-day courses cost about £100 inclusive of board, lodging and tuition. Reductions are available to the low-waged, unemployed, students and pensioners. There are facilities for physically disabled students. The course tutors include some of the best-known writers in the country, like P. D. James and Stan Barstow. You can get full details of current and projected courses on request.

The **Writers' Summer School**, Swanwick, is a six-day annual event. This is the oldest established of the writers' conferences, having begun in 1949. There are about 300 places, but it's always oversubscribed, so you should apply early. The conference is held in August, and attracts top writers as tutors and speakers. Details and application form sent on request.

The **National Institute of Adult Continuing Education (NIACE)** issues a comprehensive handbook every six months, giving the half-year's list of residential short courses held at various locations. NIACE will send you the handbook for a small charge — it includes many creative writing courses.

**Network Scotland Limited** supplies information on creative writing classes throughout Scotland, as well as information on courses leading to qualifications in literature and journalism. Each enquiry is dealt with as it comes, as the information is extensive and changes frequently. You can enquire by phone or letter, or if you live within reach of Glasgow you can take advantage of their 'drop-in' facility, for a personal meeting. Network Scotland will also send you a leaflet about their **education information services**.

**London Media Workshops** run workshops and courses on writing for radio, TV, video and the press. The courses last from one to five days, and cost from £40 to £175. The tutors and speakers are drawn from the top people working in these media. You can arrange to have your name put on the mailing list for **workshops information** and the **postal books service**, which includes many writers' manuals.

## Contact your Regional Arts Council

Ask the office of your nearest **Regional Arts Council** — your library will have the address, or look it up in the *Writers' & Artists' Yearbook* — to put your name on their regular mailing list of literary events: Writers-on-Tour, readings, workshops, information about material, including books, published locally. (Local small publishers are often interested in work by local writers.)

## Correspondence courses

The value of correspondence courses is the subject of ongoing debate in the writers' magazines. One magazine conducted a survey among its readers and found that the success or failure of the courses appeared to depend almost entirely on the calibre of the tutors. The response from course students, past and current, also indicated that the chances of a student being allocated a competent and helpful tutor are no more than fifty–fifty. When you consider the high cost, this is not encouraging.

Success with such a course, then, would appear to be as much a matter of luck as of hard work on the student's part, but nevertheless the courses attract large numbers of hopeful writers.

**The Writing School** offers a comprehensive course covering the whole range of creative writing at a cost of £149 cash plus the 'Save £30' voucher sent to prospective students. If you pay by instalments, this voucher is not valid, so the cost is £179. The student is allocated a tutor who sees him or her through all the stages of the course, which includes such varying disciplines as writing for children, for radio and TV, for the trade and technical journals, and writing a novel. Details on request.

**The London School of Journalism** offers tuition in a variety of disciplines taught in separate courses. You can choose your own specialty here, from courses in short-story writing, journalism, writing for children, writing for television, writing for radio and so on. The courses cost from £78 to £173 (cash prices). Instalment payments add up to about £10 more per course. Details on application.

There are also specialist correspondence courses on writing for children and on writing technical material — see the appropriate chapters.

## Degree courses

There are courses offering an MA degree in writing. These are by no means cheap, but you might qualify for a grant or sponsorship. The universities concerned will advise you.

**The University of Lancaster** has an MA course in Creative Writing. This is not a course for beginners, and applicants should normally have a first degree in a humanities subject. The course is either full-time (one year) or part-time (two years). Students must submit a folder of creative work, preferably typed, with their application. This is a practical course in developing writing skills and self-expression, with advice on how to get your work published. The fees are about £1,800 for the full-time course, £900 for the part-time course. Full details on request.

The **University of East Anglia** offers a post-graduate MA in Creative Writing. This is a full-time course to develop your creative and critical skills, and is not intended for the absolute beginner. You'll be asked to submit some written work for assessment with your application. The course tutors include Angela Carter and Malcolm Bradbury. You'll also be asked to show proof of financial stability. The course costs home graduate and EC (European Community) students about £2,000, and the university estimates that you'll need funds totalling about £6,000 for the year unless you can get a grant — but there's fierce competition for these. Full details of the course, and the current costs, will be sent on request.

The **University of Essex** offers an MA in Women Writing. This is a study of women's writing with the emphasis on the literature rather than the historical–sociological context in which it has been or is being written. Course details and costs will be sent on request.

## Private tutorial courses

When you attend a few writers' group meetings and read some writers' magazines, you'll come across information about privately run **tutorial and criticism services**. Many of these are run by experienced writers who want to share their know-how with aspiring writers. However, before you commit yourself, it's worth asking the editor of your favourite writers' magazine if anything is known about them. The editor will be happy to advise you, and possibly to recommend a tutor, provided you send an SAE.

## And a place for work

**The London Writing Rooms** will rent rooms to writers. For between £20 and £28 per week you can rent a private room, twenty-four hours a day, three hundred and sixty-five days a year, with your own key, the use of a kitchen, and a telephone for out-going calls only. If you can interest a few fellow writers who live within reach of London, you might think about organising a 'time-share' letting.

## For blind and partially sighted writers

**The Blind Authors' Association** offers advice, encouragement and tuition to blind and partially sighted writers. The details are given in the section **Associations and Societies Open to Unpublished Writers** on page 152.

## THE ENTERPRISE ALLOWANCE SCHEME

Are you unemployed? Would you like to have a shot at being a full-time writer? You might be able to persuade the government to support you while you try, through the **Enterprise Allowance Scheme (EAS)** run by the Manpower Services Commission.

To qualify, you must be over eighteen years of age, and you must satisfy the EAS team of interviewers that:

● You've been unemployed and receiving unemployment or supplementary benefit for at least eight weeks at the time you apply.

● You have £1,000 available to invest in your business. This can be a private loan, or a bank loan or overdraft — your bank manager will advise you.

Then, to be allowed to start a writing business, you must show the EAS team that:

● You have a clear concept of what you're going to write. You should supply, with your application, an outline of your subject, giving details of your proposed research, a business plan and an estimated timetable. (They don't appear to be very keen on high-risk, long-term projects like novels.)

● You are committed to writing full-time.

● You haven't already had work published, or tried to get work published, or already completed research — there appears to be a bit of leeway here with regard to work published or submitted for publication more than a year previously, but it seems to vary from team to team. The essential thing is to convince the interviewers that what you're starting is a brand new business.

You'll be required to attend at least one seminar, and be interviewed by a bank manager and a business advisory consultant. If you satisfy all the requirements, the Manpower Services Commission will pay you £40 a week for a year.

You'll have access to a back-up business advisory service. The usefulness and efficiency of this varies, apparently, from one part of the country to another, so it might be as well to cultivate your friendly bank manager for his advice as well as his money.

### It's a big step
Writer John Brown, who lives in Manchester, started on the scheme in July 1987. He was then 37, and redundancy had put him out of work early in 1986. John is married and has three young children. Applying for the Enterprise Allowance was a big step, for he knew he'd probably be far better off on the dole. But he'd been bitten by the writing bug when he saw 'Only Fools and Horses' on TV, and thought he would love to be able to write something as good as that. He decided to

concentrate on writing comedy material, so he joined the Comedy Writers Association.

Being funny is hard work, but John is getting there. He's sold material to BBC TV ('Alas Smith and Jones' and 'What's All This Then?') and Granada TV ('The Grumbleweeds'), as well as to German TV and radio. He's sold ideas for greeting cards, and is now trying to break into the lucrative American market. The cheques are still irregular, but are coming in more often now.

John advises '...Don't get to fifty or sixty and wish you'd had a go. With the help of the EAS, you can do it now...even if it's only for a year.'

Ask at your local Job Centre for details of the Enterprise Allowance Scheme. They have leaflets available, and will advise you on how to apply.

**Could you double your money?**

If your husband or wife or another member of your family can legitimately apply for and be approved by the Enterprise Scheme as your secretary, the partnership would receive an income of £80 per week for a year. Could you qualify? The second member must be a full partner in your business, and you must *both* satisfy the conditions of entry. That is, you must *both* have been unemployed and signing on for at least eight weeks, and you must be able to show that you have £1,000 *each* to put in the business. You should then present a joint business plan.

Richard Halford made a successful application on behalf of himself and his wife. His wife's part in the business plan is:

●   to work full time as Richard's secretary — typist, book-keeper, clerk and so on — so that Richard is free to concentrate on the creative side of the writing;

●   to be responsible for typing final copies of all material ready for submission to the markets;

●   to be responsible for sending that material out and keeping records of it;

●   to keep all stationery supplies stocked up.

Richard submitted this plan, and was asked to supply a breakdown of his wife's proposed working hours. The joint plan was then accepted, and the Halfords are now working together, in partnership, with a total allowance of £80 per week.

If you intend to make a success of your creative talent, it will pay to give attention, too, to the practical aspect of the writing business — keeping records.

| CHECKLIST |
|-----------|
| Start drawing up a plan of action. Here are a few basic first steps — you can add to them as your knowledge grows and your ambitions begin to focus. |

| Objective | How to achieve it |
|-----------|-------------------|
| 1. Begin to learn about the writing business. | Buy, or borrow from the library, *Writing for Pleasure and Profit* (Michael Legat) and *The Writing Business* (Liz Taylor). |
| 2. If you can't already type, take action to learn. | Buy or borrow a reasonably good machine. Buy a typing manual or arrange tuition. |
| 3. Join (or initiate) a writers' group. | Make enquiries at the library. Advertise for other writers to make contact. |
| 4. Begin to get to know the pleasures and problems you'll have in common with other writers, both new and experienced. | Send for a copy of at least one writers' magazine. |
| 5. Start to whet your appetite for eventual publication. | Buy and *read through* the *Writers' & Artists' Yearbook* or *The Writer's Handbook* — both, if you can. |

## KEEPING RECORDS

To keep your writing affairs in order, it's best to start making simple records right at the beginning. Note everything down as it happens. If you leave it till the end of the month — or even the end of the week — you'll probably forget something. You need the following:

1. **A cash book**, to record expenditure. Note every penny spent, including the purchase of this book, and keep the receipts in a file. Note, too, *any* money you earn from your writing, no matter how small the sum.

2.  **A record book**, to keep track of your articles, stories, poems —
    where you send them, whether they're accepted or rejected, paid
    for or not and so on.
3.  **A markets book**, to record your dealings with individual markets.
    Keep detailed notes as you gather information and experience of
    each one. List every item you send there, and keep a record of its
    progress. Note how you found that market to deal with — friendly
    or off-hand, prompt or slow, efficient or not... Note changes in
    editorial personnel, policy and so on, anything that might be useful
    in future dealings there (even if it's only 'Never again!').
4.  **A 'writing only' diary**, or a set of labelled folders, or some other
    system suited to your particular type of writing. You need to keep
    track of deadlines, seasonal material, forthcoming competitions and
    the like.

### The cash book
Anything legitimately spent on your writing business — on equipment,
stationery, stamps, books and magazines, phone calls, subscriptions,
travelling expenses and so on — could be tax-deductible against future
earnings, and you might be asked to produce receipts to support your
claims.

By law, you must declare your earnings, however modest, in each financial year. The only exception *at present* is that competition prizes are not taxable.

If you spend a lot on postage — and most writers do — it's a good idea to keep a separate postage book, to log details of out-going letters and packages. Enter purchases of stamps and IRCs and postage on packets in your cash book. Log individual letters and other items posted, with their destinations and dates of posting and so on, in your postage book. In this way, you'll have to account (to yourself) for every stamp you use, so you won't be tempted to raid your 'writing' stamps for other letters.

| 1988 | | | | 1988 | | | |
|---|---|---|---|---|---|---|---|
| June | | £ | p | June | | £ | p |
| 2 | 2 ribbons | 3 | 90 | 9 | Reader's letter *(Woman)* | 5 | 00 |
| | 1 pkt paper clips | | 45 | 21 | Article: *The Lady* | 38 | 00 |
| | 1 ream bond paper | 5 | 95 | | | | |
| | 1 pkt Tipp-Ex strips | 1 | 50 | | | | |
| | (John Jotter Ltd) | | | | | | |
| 11 | 20 × 13p stamps | 2 | 60 | | | | |
| | 6 × 20p stamps | 1 | 20 | | | | |
| | Book: *The Writing Business* | 3 | 95 | | | | |
| | (Bookbuff & Co) | | | | | | |
| 14 | Sub renewal *(Success)* | 10 | 00 | | | | |
| 17 | Photocopying *Bees* article | | 50 | | | | |

Example: two facing pages from a cash book.

The accepted book-keeping practice is to record debit (money spent) entries on the left-hand page, and credit (money received) entries on the facing right-hand page.

## The record book

A loose-leaf book is best for this. You can add pages as you need them. Keep a page for each item you write. You'll be able to see at a glance what's happening to each story, article or poem.

| Item: Short story     Title: 'A Listening Ear'     Length: 1,600 words | | | | |
|---|---|---|---|---|
| Date sent | Sent to | Accepted/ rejected | Payment received | Date |
| 31.5.87 | *Woman's Weekly* | Rejected | — | 22.6.87 |
| 25.9.87 | *Christian Herald* | Accepted | £23.00 | 5.2.88 |

Example: page from a record book

## The markets book

Keep a page for each target market, and list every item you send to that market. This is a simple system, easy to keep up to date, and it will help you to avoid misdirected or duplicated submissions.

| *Woman's Dream* 11 Milky Way Starville XX7 7XX | | | | Editor: ~~Livia Lush~~ Verity Verucca | | |
|---|---|---|---|---|---|---|
| Date sent | Item | Accepted/ rejected | Payment received | Date | Remarks | |
| 27.9.87 | Short story: *Alien Love* | Accepted | £50.00 | 22.2.88 | Prompt payment on publication. Voucher copy. Nice note from editor asking for more. | |
| 17.3.88 | Short story: *The Gemini Factor* | Rejected 21.3.88 | — | — | Sudden change of editor. No note with rejection slip. Hold this one till new policy clear. | |

Example: page from a markets book

Before putting pen to paper there are still some important matters to consider, which often appear to budding writers more forbidding than they need be — copyright, plagiarism and libel.

## COPYRIGHT

**Copyright** simply means 'the right to copy'. No one but you has the right to reproduce, print, publish or sell any part of your writing unless you grant them permission to do so. The law protects your copyright during your lifetime and for fifty years after your death. The copyright is your property, and you can sell it if you wish, outright and for a lump sum, but you would then be giving up all further claim on it, and would have absolutely no right to any money made from that work in the future.

You don't have to register your copyright. It belongs to you the minute you set your words down on paper. (This even applies to personal letters. The *letter* belongs to the recipient, but the *words* it contains still belong to you, and no one has the right to publish them without your written consent.)

The copyright line you see in books and magazines — the author's name preceded by the sign © — is a warning to the public that the work is protected. There's no need to put this line on your ms — your work is already protected, and it's highly unlikely that a publisher would steal your material.

However, if you're at all worried about your copyright being infringed even before you see your work in print, you can protect yourself quite easily. Just send a copy of your ms to yourself by registered post, then take the unopened package and your receipt (make sure the date is clear) to a safe place like a bank. Deposit it, and get a receipt there as well. You'll then have concrete proof, if for any reason you have to prove when your ms was written.

### If you're tempted to sell your copyright...
You can sell your material outright if you wish, for a fixed one-off payment. However, you should avoid doing this if you can, even if the wolf has a foot and a half inside your door. You don't know what goodies you might be signing away. When the Nazis occupied Austria, an aristocratic family fled to America. Hungry, disoriented and unsure of their future, they sold their story for the price of a few weeks' food and lodging. They signed away their copyright, and with it all future claims on the story. The family's name was Von Trapp, and their story became the multi-million-dollar musical *The Sound of Music*. The Von Trapps didn't get another cent.

## The copyright laws operate both ways

Just as your work is protected from other writers' plundering, so their work is protected from you. You can't use other people's writings without their consent, that is you can't quote any substantial part of another writer's work without written permission. And that permission can be expensive. The recommendations of the Society of Authors and the Publishers Association for basic minimum fees for quotation and anthology use, published in *The Author*, Winter 1987 issue, are:

- prose (world rate) £70–£82 per 1,000 words;
- poetry (world rate) £52–£62 for ten lines, £26–£31 for each succeeding ten lines or less.

### 'Fair dealing'

This term is used to describe the legitimate use of published material 'for purposes of criticism or review'. This is generally interpreted as meaning that you can quote a line or two to illustrate a point you want to make, *provided you give due acknowledgement of the source of the quotation.*

For example, in this book, in the chapter on writing articles, two short sentences are quoted from Gordon Wells's book *The Craft of Writing Articles* to reinforce a point made in that chapter. Both the author's name and the name of the book are stated there. This is 'fair dealing'. On the other hand, the paragraph quoted from Liz Taylor's book *The Writing Business*, at the beginning of this book, is printed with the author's *written* permission. It would have been discourteous, to say the least, to reproduce Liz Taylor's words in such a prominent way without her permission, and she would have had good cause for complaint.

We shouldn't forget the gaffe made by Princess Michael of Kent when she wrote her book *Crowned in a Far Country*, and used large chunks of other authors' works without any acknowledgements at all.

It would be safer, then, till you're more familiar with the not too well defined legal niceties, either to avoid quoting from other authors altogether, or to seek permission for *anything* you want to use. Your request for permission, by the way, should normally be sent to the publishers, not directly to the author.

### Co-authorship

The rule protecting copyright for fifty years after an author's death also applies to writing partnerships, such as an artist collaborating with an author to produce an illustrated book, a lyric-writer and a composer pooling their talents to write a song, or two authors writing a book together. The work concerned doesn't come out of copyright and into the public domain — that is, free for use by anyone — until a full fifty years after the death of the last surviving partner.

So don't assume that because one half of a writing team has been dead for the statutory fifty years his work is automatically free of copyright protection. There was an expensive example of this trap in the 1960s, involving the famous partnership of Gilbert and Sullivan, who wrote the Savoy Operas. Pye Records made a jazz album, 'The Coolest Mikado', based on Sir Arthur Sullivan's music for *The Mikado*. Pye released the record in 1961, but were obliged to withdraw it almost immediately at a huge financial loss. (If you come across one of the copies that were sold before the ban, it's a collector's item.)

Sullivan had died in 1900, so his fifty-years-after-death were long up. But W. S. Gilbert didn't die till 1911. The jazz arrangements were written and the recording made before *Gilbert's* copyright ran out, and his copyright protected Sullivan's music. Pye had infringed the joint copyright.

## PLAGIARISM

**Plagiarism** is the use without permission, for your own purposes, of work in which the copyright is held by someone else. There's no copyright in plots, ideas or titles, but you could have problems if, for instance, you follow someone else's story-line so closely that there's a recognisable connection.

In 1987, the estate of Margaret Mitchell brought a complaint of plagiarism against the French author Régine Desforges, in America. Mme Desforges's novel trilogy, published in English as *The Blue Bicycle* trilogy, is pretty clearly recognisable as a re-telling of *Gone With The Wind* in a World War Two setting. The plot and the principal characters have more than a passing resemblance to those of the famous Civil War novel. Mme Desforges has never denied that the American novel provided the inspiration for her books, but she's being sued nevertheless.

You could have problems, too, if you called your book *Catch 22* or *The Eagle Has Landed*. Although there's no copyright in titles, this could be claimed to be a deliberate attempt to mislead.

## LIBEL

**Libel** is a statement made in print or in writing, or broadcast on radio or television, which defames the character of an identifiable living person by holding them up to hatred, contempt or ridicule.

Don't be caught out by an unintentional libel. If you make recognisable use, for instance, of a public figure (or even your next-door neighbour) as the model for a character who commits a criminal act, you could be inviting a libel suit.

The same caution applies to the use of names. If you call one of your characters David Owen, make him a GP who has gone into politics, and then have him drop a spot of arsenic into the Prime Minister's coffee, the good doctor would have a pretty strong case against you.

The Society of Authors' *Quick Guides* series of leaflets includes guides to copyright and libel. They cost £1 each, direct from the Society.

# 2
# Preparing and Submitting Your Work

## WHERE WILL YOU SEND YOUR MANUSCRIPT?

You should have a clear idea of your target market *before* you begin to write an article or a story. Too many new writers — and some who should know better — write the piece, revise it, polish it up and prepare the ms, *then* start looking for a suitable outlet.

Successful writers seldom work that way. They write with a specific market in mind, a market they've already studied in detail. They tailor the content, treatment, style and length of the work to suit that market.

### Market study is just common sense

There's no great mystique about it. Think of your writing as a product you're making for sale. No, don't frown and say you couldn't possibly think of creative writing in that way. If you want to sell your work, you *must* think like that. You're entering a business transaction, little different from selling birdseed or a three-piece suite. You are the manufacturer, and you have to supply what the retailer wants. An editor is a retailer. He buys from the manufacturer — the writer — what he knows he can sell to his customers — his readers.

The editor of *Woman's Weekly* won't buy a fantasy-horror story. She knows she would lose readers. Mills & Boon won't buy a science fiction novel. It's not what their customers expect from them. A literary magazine would have no slot for a DIY article. Yet misdirected mss like that boost Post Office profits year after year.

At the very least, make sure that your ms is targeted at the right area of publishing, an area that publishes *that kind* of material.

## SELECTING A MARKET

Start by studying the *Writers' & Artists' Yearbook* and *The Writer's*

*Handbook*. Read right through the section you're interested in —
magazines, newspapers, book publishers, radio and television, theatrical
producers, wherever your particular interest lies. Don't just look up the
names you know. There might be potential markets you haven't even
heard of before.

Select a few that seem appropriate, and take a serious, analytical look
at them to see what prospects they hold for you, as a new freelance
writer. This will give you a useful starting point.

These two writers' manuals, however, don't list all the possible
markets. Later in the book you'll find specific sources of information
about markets in the various fields. For the moment, let's look at the
general principles of market study.

*'Well, I've found a market, but where did I put my story?'*

**Shoot with a rifle — not with a shotgun**

1. Make sure, *before you send anything,* that the market you want to sell to is willing to consider unsolicited contributions.
2. Make sure that the content, treatment and style of your work is suitable for your target market.
3. Make sure that the length of the piece complies with the publisher's stated word limits.

Let's look at these points in detail, because if you get any of them wrong you won't only lose a possible sale, you might damage your credibility. Careless marketing warns an editor that you're not taking your business seriously.

**1.  Are unsolicited mss welcome?**

Start with the publication itself. Look at the small print at the front or near the end. Many magazines print statements like 'No responsibility taken for unsolicited mss' indicating that such mss will at least be read, or 'No unsolicited mss' meaning that they won't. The *Writers' & Artists' Yearbook* and *The Writer's Handbook* give a good general guide to whether or not you'll be wasting your time with unsolicited material. Some of the writers' magazines, particularly *Success*, carry regular features on current editorial wants, and *Freelance Market News* has news of current and upcoming markets (you should check this at source — the information isn't always complete).

The only one hundred per cent reliable source of information is the publisher's own editorial department. If you have any doubts about their willingness at least to read your unsolicited ms, ask them.

Write a *brief* letter to the editorial department:

---

Dear sir (or 'Dear madam' if it's a feminist publisher)

Do you consider unsolicited material? If you do, would you please send me any available guidelines for writers, or advise me of any subject areas not open to freelances. I enclose a stamped addressed envelope. Thank you.

Yours sincerely

---

Don't forget the SAE. And be patient — publishing offices get a lot of mail. Don't ask for free sample copies 'to study your requirements'. If it's a trade publication, or one you can't find in the shops, ask if they'll send you a copy or two and invoice you for them. If they do invoice you, pay up. Your market study is your responsibility, not the publisher's. It's neither reasonable nor professional to ask another business to subsidise yours.

You can get a quicker answer to your problem, of course, if you ring up the editorial office. Most publishers don't mind this, so long as you don't engage them in a long conversation about your work, or generally take up a lot of time. Just ask to speak to someone in the editorial office if it's a magazine, or ask for the appropriate department if you're ringing a publishing house.

It's a good idea to prepare a short list of questions before you phone, so that you get *all* the answers you need without wasting time trying to remember them off the cuff. The kind of questions you'll probably want to ask are, for example:

1.  Do you welcome unsolicited material from freelance writers?
2.  Are there any subjects that are written by your staff only?
3.  What lengths do you prefer?
4.  Do you prefer an enquiry first, or would you rather see the whole ms?
5.  Do you have any guidelines I could send for?

Note down, too, any other questions you might want to ask about a particular market. For example, you could take the opportunity, if you already know what you plan to write for them, of asking for the name of the appropriate editor, so that you can address your work or your enquiry to him or her by name.

Don't go into any detail about what you're writing unless they ask you. Be as brief and business-like as you can. All you need at this stage is basic information.

### 2. Is your material suitable?
The first and most essential point to establish is that your subject matter is acceptable and appropriate. As a beginner, you might feel most secure in this if you stick to familiar ground. That is, if you write for publications you already know and like, at least till you have some experience. That old writers' adage, 'write about what you know', could be a valuable guide to you here.

You know why *you* buy your favourite magazines, you're familiar with their tone and outlook, so you won't be likely to send them something you wouldn't want to find there yourself. You'd be pretty surprised, wouldn't you, to find a feature on building a drystone wall in *Punch* or a piece on watercolour painting in *Practical Photography*. You wouldn't be likely, then, to send such features to these publications.

Yet, believe it or not, people do that kind of thing all the time.

You should be sure, then, that *at the very least* you choose a market that's compatible with what you want to write.

## Getting the tone and language right

The next step is to get hold of a few *recent* copies of your target publisher's products. (It can be worse than useless to use even last year's issues, because editorial policies change frequently.) Make out a study sheet, and analyse the publication, noting down *all* the points that strike you.

1. What kind of people are likely to read this publication?
   Age range?
   Sex?
   Types of occupation?
   Their interests and hobbies?
   Their aims and ambitions?

2. Why would they want to read this particular publication?
   For pleasure and relaxation?
   For instruction?

3. Can you detect a clear editorial policy or attitude? Is the publication delivering any kind of message to its readers?

4. What kind of topics and subjects are used in the publication?

5. Are there any topics *not* covered that you might have expected to see there?

6. What areas *appear* to be written by staff members?

The last point is one which might be deceptive to even the most experienced writer. You'll often come across market information and advice that uses terms like 'appears to be staff-written', or 'this looks as if there could be an opening for the freelance'. You should treat this kind of advice very cautiously. Things are not always what they seem. One editor remarked, in response to an enquiry from a writer's magazine about his requirements, that a series he was running was indeed staff-written, but *only because* no freelance had ever offered him anything on that subject, and he was keen to cover it. This is one area where you can only trust 'horse's-mouth' information. Ask the editorial office.

You'll get a lot of help with your answers to these questions if you study the advertisements in the publication. They can give you strong clues about the interests, concerns and age range of the readers.

## Look at the language

Now add a section to your analysis sheet in which you look at the language that's used in the publication. The kind of questions you should ask are:

1. Are the words short and simple?
2. Or more sophisticated and multi-syllable?
3. Are the sentences short and simply constructed, with few subordinate clauses?
4. Or are they fairly complex in structure?
5. Is the general tone formal or casual?
6. Are the words, for the most part, formal or colloquial?

The advertisements can help with this too, because they give you a picture in your mind of the kind of people you'll be writing for.

If you pitch the tone and language either too high or too low, you'll have less chance of producing a totally suitable piece of writing. Gordon Wells has a very detailed section on market analysis in his book *The Craft of Writing Articles*. Read it if you can.

## 3. Have you got the length right?

Most of the publications and book publishers listed in the *Writers' & Artists' Yearbook* specify the minimum and/or maximum number of words they want for each submission. There's no point in ignoring these word limits. Editors have a certain amount of space to fill, and they won't alter either their policy or the size of their product to accommodate, say, a 3,000 word story if their stated limit is 2,000 words. And they can't tape the excess wordage on to the back cover.

You'll see how to calculate your wordage in the section on preparing your mss.

## Keep up to date

You're going into a business that's never static. Magazines vanish, new ones appear. Big publishers eat up small ones. Rebels set up on their own. Editors move about, and often take their pet policies with them, so that their 'new' magazine might quickly become indistinguishable from their last one.

Don't rely on reference books that are even a year or two out of date. You could waste far more money on misdirected mss than it would cost you to replace your out-of-date information sources.

Before you send anything off, then, be sure that:

● what you're sending is suitable to the best of your judgement for the publication you're sending it to;

- you've written the piece in an appropriate style;
- your ms complies with the publication's stated word limits;
- the publication is willing to consider it;
- your market research is bang up to date.

## SHOULD YOU TRY AN AGENT?

Raise the topic of agents at any writers' gathering and you can expect heated argument all round. The most common comment heard from unpublished or little-published writers is that 'agents don't want to know you till you've already made it'.

This might be true as far as some agents are concerned, but it's far more likely that these disappointed writers have had their work rejected by an agent for the same reason most mss are rejected by publishers. They just aren't good enough to publish. An agent won't take on the job of trying to place a book that he or she has no confidence in, any more than a publisher will accept a book he knows he can't sell.

A good agent chooses his clients very carefully, because he'll be committing himself to a lot of work on their behalf. If you can place your work with a competent agent, you'll establish a working partnership that will be mutually profitable. The agent will secure you better terms from most publishers, and will have enough knowledge of the markets, both at home and overseas, to see that the rights in your book are exploited as fully as possible. Yes, the agent gets ten per cent of the profits — but *you* get ninety per cent, and that could mean ninety per cent of sales you wouldn't have got without the agent's know-how.

Do try to place your work with an agent if you want to, but be realistic about it. Your chances of a favourable response are just about the same as your chances of acceptance by a publisher. Neither will want a substandard piece of work.

There are lists of agents in the *Writers' & Artists' Yearbook* and *The Writer's Handbook*. Choose one who handles the kind of work you've written, otherwise you'll have no chance at all. Most agents listed state how they prefer to be approached — by letter, or by sending a synopsis, or by sending the full ms.

Dorothy Lumley runs the **Dorian Literary Agency**. She handles full-length fiction; as well as mainstream novels, she has a special interest in crime, thrillers, romance, historical and sagas, science fiction, fantasy and horror. Dorothy also takes full-length adult non-fiction. She only considers short stories by authors whose books she handles, and takes no poetry or scripts. She works with agents for translation. There is no reading fee. Commission: UK 10%, US 15%, translation usually 20%. Please contact Dorothy by letter first, with SAE.

When contacting an agent please give as much information as possible, i.e. whether you already have one and wish to change, a CV of your published works to date, and what you want to write in future. An editor only wants to let an ms speak for itself, an agent wants to know how you view your writing career. If you received any comments on a current ms from an editor who has rejected it, it's useful to pass these on to any agent you approach.

Dorothy Lumley.

The partnership of Jane Gregory and Lisanne Radice runs two literary agencies, both with a special interest in new authors: **Gregory and Radice, Authors' Agents**, handles *only* crime and thrillers, with a particular interest in stories with a political edge; **The Jane Gregory Agency** handles fiction and non-fiction full-length mss. Neither agency handles short stories, original film scripts, plays, academic or children's books. New authors are given encouragement and editorial advice. There's no reading fee. Both agencies require a preliminary letter, with SAE.

**Diane Burston** is one of the few agents who will handle short stories from other than established clients (see Chapter 8).

The **Society of Authors** publishes a *Quick Guide to Authors' Agents* (No. 9).

## OVERSEAS MARKETS

The whole English-speaking world is open to you. Some of the overseas markets are listed in the *Writers' & Artists' Yearbook*, and *Freelance Market News* carries a quarterly supplement, 'Selling Abroad', which lists current overseas openings and their requirements.

### The USA

The biggest and most lucrative market is the United States of America. The potential for sales there is enormous. With material for the American markets, however, the marketing strategy is more clearly defined than in the UK. It's universal practice to send a query letter or a proposal first, *not* a complete ms. 'Over the transom' (unsolicited) submissions are vigorously discouraged. Many publishers don't even open the packages — they simply mark them 'Return to sender'.

## Writers' guidelines

Before you send *anything*, even a query letter, your first move should be to write to your chosen target magazines and ask for their **writers' guidelines**. US magazines issue these as standard practice. It's essential to enclose International Reply Coupons with your request.

These guidelines are very useful. They describe the magazine's requirements in detail, and tell you what the editors want and how they want you to send it. They're designed to save time and expense for both the magazine and its would-be contributors.

### Writer's Market

You'll find the US markets (about 4,000 of them) listed in the annual *Writer's Market*. This is a hardback book, well over 1,000 pages long, and includes many articles and tips on freelance writing as well as information about the markets. The information it gives is comprehensive and detailed. You're left in no doubt at all about the suitability of the markets to your needs, and vice versa.

*Writer's Market* is published by Writer's Digest Books, and you can buy it by mail order from **Freelance Press Services**. It costs about US $22, the UK price depending on the current exchange rate. (The 1988 issue cost £16.50 post paid.) Freelance Press Services will send you current prices on request. They can also arrange subscriptions to the two main American writers' magazines, *Writer's Digest* and *The Writer*.

### Tips on writing for the US market

1. Always send for guidelines first.
2. At the same time, ask for a copy of the magazine, and enclose enough IRCs to pay for it and for the return postage. Many of the magazines listed in *Writer's Market* tell you how many IRCs to send.
3. Study the sample magazine carefully for style.
4. Invest in a dictionary of American spellings — it's essential that you write your material in 'American' English.

## WRITING SEASONAL AND ANNIVERSARY MATERIAL

### Seasonal material

**Seasonal material** is the term used to describe a book, story, article, poem, song or greeting card whose subject matter relates to a particular season of the year: Christmas, Easter, Hallowe'en and so on.

Seasonal material has to be sent well in advance, anything from three months to a year or even more. It's no use waiting till October to submit a Christmas story to a magazine — the Christmas issue will be ready to print by then.

If you don't already have guidelines which include this information from your target publication, you must check their seasonal deadlines. The quickest and easiest way (all round) to do this is to phone the editorial department and ask. No one will mind this, provided you're brief and businesslike.

**Insider tip 1.** Write your seasonal pieces *during* the season. It can be hard to get into a 'mistletoe and holly' mood when you're drooping over a hot sticky keyboard on a sweltering summer's day. File the piece away, and make a careful note to remind you when to send it off. Get it out a few days early, and give it an objective, critical reading. You might see faults you didn't notice when you wrote it, and you'll have time now to put them right and to give the work that final polish that can make the difference between a sale and a rejection.

**Insider tip 2.** Avoid including any reference to current events, unless your piece is intended to be relevant to that year only. Topical references will make it unsaleable in future years.

### Anniversary material

**Anniversary material** is anything on the theme of a past event, written for publication on or near an anniversary of that event. Like seasonal material, anniversary pieces must be submitted well in advance of the relevant date, especially if the event being commemorated is well known and widely documented. As a beginner, you would probably be wasting your time writing about D-Day or a Royal birthday, for instance, unless you've unearthed something new and/or sensational. You could try sending a query letter, but you're likely to find that your target magazine already has something on the subject either in stock or commissioned from a regular contributor or from a famous 'name'.

The *Writers' & Artists' Yearbook* prints a useful Journalists' Calendar of up-coming anniversaries.

Your local papers and magazines might like features about the anniversaries of interesting local people and events, especially if you can link them to something that's happening today. Working from local knowledge, you can start researching early enough to offer the editor a feature packed with facts and human interest — and that's the kind that sells.

### HOW TO PREPARE YOUR MANUSCRIPT

There's a standard layout that you should always follow when you're typing short stories, articles or books. (Poetry, playscript and picture-script layouts are shown in the relevant chapters later.) A well presented ms could increase your chances of acceptance. A slovenly one could destroy them.

### First impressions count

Your ms says a lot about *you*. Give an editor a crisp, clean, well set out ms, with accurate spelling, grammar and punctuation, and you give him reason to have at least some confidence in its content, even before he's read it. You've shown him that you care about what you're doing, and that you're approaching the job in a professional way. And even if he doesn't want this piece, you'll have banked some goodwill for the future.

A sloppy ms won't get a warm welcome. Don't imagine that the editor will toil manfully through a scruffy script, ignoring coffee stains, over-typings, blisters of Tipp-ex, your bald ribbon or your ink-starved dot-matrix printer, in a tireless quest for literary genius. He won't. He might not bother to read much of it at all, because he'll judge, probably accurately, that you won't handle any of your business efficiently.

You're offering your work for sale in a highly competitive market. Don't turn your customers off with tatty packaging.

Don't rush it. When you've done a complete draft:

- Check your spelling, grammar, punctuation and syntax.
- Alter any clumsy phrasing or repetitions.
- Check that all personal and place names are accurate and consistent. Page one's brown-eyed Babs mustn't have blue eyes on page five, either, so check that your descriptions are consistent, too.
- Check *any* facts you're not absolutely sure about. If an editor spots the smallest inaccuracy of fact, he'll start to worry that there might be a big one somewhere.
- **Insider tip:** When you've read each page for its sense, read it again line by line *from the bottom up*, covering the lines below as you go. This is a proofreader's trick that throws up mis-spellings you can easily miss in a straight reading.
- Finally, check the word count — see below. As you've seen when you read about market study, you should be working with a particular market in mind, certainly by this stage. Make sure *now* that you don't need to cut any excess wordage.

### Calculating your wordage

You should understand that counting every word does *not* give an accurate assessment of the number of printed pages your ms will need. Look at the text of a book or magazine. You'll see that while most of the lines occupy the full width of the text many do not. Take, for example, lines like:

She looked up.
'Oh no,' she sighed.
'It's true.'

Here you have just nine words — and they use up three lines.

You can see, then, what a distorted picture you'll get if you just count words. You should treat *every* line, however short, as a full line, including the last lines of paragraphs. Think of the whole text area as solid with words.

This is how to do it:

1. Count the exact number of words in fifty full-length lines. Divide that number by fifty. This gives the average number of words per line.
2. Add up the total number of lines in your ms — if it's a novel, take the average number of lines per page over ten full pages, and multiply by the total number of pages in the ms — count short pages at the beginning and end of chapters as full pages.
3. Now multiply the average number of words per line by the total number of pages.

Here's an example:

| | | |
|---|---|---:|
| Total number of words in 50 full lines | = | 710 |
| Average number of words per line = 710/50 | = | 14.2 |
| Total number of pages in the ms | = | 193 |
| Average number of lines per page | = | 28 |
| Total number of lines in the ms = 193 x 28 | = | 5,404 |
| Total number of words = 5,404 x 14.2 | = | 76,736.8 |

You would then round this figure *up* to the nearest thousand, so your final word count, the one you would type on your ms, would be 'About 77,000 words'.

## Make it beautiful

Use good quality plain **white A4 bond paper** for your top copy. It will have to stand up to a lot of handling and editorial marking if your ms is accepted. Keep a carbon copy (bank paper is adequate for this), but don't send a carbon to the editor. A good photocopy is usually acceptable.

Make sure your typewriter ribbon is good enough to produce a clear, sharp, black, **easy-to-read type**. Use *only* a black ribbon, and avoid fancy typefaces (gothic, italic, script and so on). A plain face is much easier to read.

Leave **good margins** all round, at least an inch, with a bit more on the left, where space will be needed for typesetting instructions. Keep your pages uniform in layout.

Type in **double spacing**. That means leaving one full line of blank space between the lines of type. It *doesn't* mean hitting the space bar twice between words. Type on one side of the paper only.

Even if your machine has the facility to do so, **don't justify** (make even) the right-hand margin. This complicates length calculations. Don't leave extra space between paragraphs, either, but do indent the first line of each paragraph so that there's no confusion about where they begin and end.

**Don't underline** anything unless you intend it to appear in italics.

### Identify your work

Put your name and address on your cover sheet *and* on the first and last pages of text. Number the pages consecutively, even for a full-length work — *don't* begin again with 'Page one' at the start of each chapter.

At the top right of each page, type your name, the title (or an abbreviation of it) and the page number. This is called a **strap-line**, and it ensures that your pages don't get out of order (or mislaid).

At the bottom right of every page except the very last, type 'mf', which means 'more follows', telling the editor and the typesetter that there's more copy to come. Underneath the last line of the last page type 'ends'.

Follow the layout as shown in the example on page 47.

### Good reasons for following conventional layouts

It really *is* essential to stick to the conventional forms of manuscript layout. These haven't come about by chance, or been chosen haphazardly. They're the layouts that publishers and printers have found to be the clearest, quickest, safest and least expensive to work on:

● **Clearest** because the double-spaced lines of plain black type on white paper are easy to read and least tiring to the copy editors' and typesetters' eyes.

● **Quickest** because the good margins and double-spaced text leave enough room for editorial corrections and typesetting instructions to be marked clearly and rapidly, and also because they speed length calculations.

```
Short story                    Patricia Brennan,
                               21 Our Street,
                               Printville,
About 1,000 words              Papershire,
                               England PS99 OXX.

                               Tel. (001) 101 101




              The Christmas Kitten

                       by

              Patricia Brennan












FBSR
```

Cover sheet.

Patricia Brennan,
21 Our Street,
Printville,
Papershire,
England PS99 OXX.

Tel. (001) 101 101

1,000 words

### The Christmas Kitten

by  Patricia Brennan

It was nearly Christmas. There was snow on the ground and it felt very cold.

A little black kitten was out all on his own. 'Miaow,' he said. 'My paws are cold and my ears are cold and all of me is cold. Oh, I do wish I had not got lost.' But there was no-one to hear the little black kitten.

He ran along a path and felt a bit warmer then. Suddenly he saw some light from a house in front of him.

'Perhaps the people there would like a kitten to live with them,' he thought, so he went towards the light. When he reached the house, he saw that the light was coming from a back door which was open. The little black kitten ran inside the house. It was warm in there and he felt so pleased that he had found this lovely house.

Suddenly there was a loud bark and a large dog charged into the kitchen. 'What are you doing here?' he said. 'Don't you know this is my house? You can't share my food. Go away with you.'

'But I am so cold and hungry,' said the kitten. 'Can I not stay with you? I won't eat much and I do need a home.'

'No, you can't,' said the dog. 'This is my home and I am not having any other animals here with me. Be off with you.'

The little black kitten went out again into the cold, dark mf

*The Christmas Kitten* was published in Lancashire's *Valley Life* magazine, December/January 1987/8. This extract is reproduced here in typescript form with Patricia Brennan's permission.

- **Safest** because their clarity, even after corrections have been marked, reduces the risk of typesetting errors or misunderstandings.
- **Least expensive** because all the foregoing points contribute to speed and accuracy, cutting the time-schedules and reducing the need for costly corrections at proof stage — and so keeping costs down and quality high.

Your observation of the preferred layouts will contribute substantially to your professional credibility.

### The cover sheet

The cover sheet for the story shown in the example on page 46 would look something like that shown. The exact layout can be varied, but the important thing is to put all the information there.

### FBSR

The abbreviation FBSR stands for First British Serial Rights, and means that you're offering the right to publish your article or story for the first time in the UK. You can only offer this right if the piece hasn't been published in the UK before — if it has, you should give the editor its publishing history in your covering letter.

The term FBSR is not used for full-length book mss.

### The final check

Before you pack up your work for posting, give it a final read through. Make any necessary corrections as neatly and clearly as you can, using a black pen. You shouldn't be making any major corrections at this stage, just tidying up minor typing errors.

## ILLUSTRATIONS

Some magazines, especially the heavily illustrated kind, won't consider articles without illustrations. You should find out what kind of illustrations are preferred before you send anything. Black and white prints should be glossy — they give a sharper reproduction than matt-finish ones. Colour pictures are usually submitted as transparencies, and should be protected by plastic covers. Pack prints between sheets of card.

Don't stick your illustrations on to the ms. Pencil *very lightly* an identification number on the back of each one, and pencil the numbers in the ms margins where you want them to go. The page layouts might make it difficult to place them exactly where you indicate, but they'll be placed as near as possible. Type captions on a separate sheet and number them to correspond with the illustration numbers.

## PEN-NAMES

You can use a pen-name if you want to. This should be shown in the byline, but *not* above your address. For instance, if Patricia Brennan had wanted *The Christmas Kitten* to appear under the name of, say, Alice Brent, she would have typed her own name and address as shown, but under the title of the story, she would have typed 'by Alice Brent'.

## HOW TO APPROACH AN EDITOR

Before we look at the best (and worst) ways of making your first approach, you can be reassured about one thing: no editor will turn down a good piece of work solely because you didn't get your method of contact exactly right first time.

Provided you communicate in a courteous, businesslike way, the editor will either consider your submitted ms anyway, or return it and advise you about the preferred approach.

### Find out what to do
It does smooth the way all round, though, if you find out and follow each editor's preferences. You can do this by:

- looking up the publication or publishing house in the *Writers' & Artists' Yearbook* or *The Writer's Handbook*, where the entry will probably give you at least a clue;
- or phoning a brief enquiry to the editorial office, asking:
  1. 'Do you prefer to see a letter, a synopsis, or the complete script in the first instance?'
  2. 'What is the name of the editor to whom I should address my submission?'

  You might also be offered some other useful information at this point, too — for instance, that the editor in question is on holiday for a month, or that there's already a large backlog of unsolicited mss waiting to be looked at.

If you can't get hold of any specific information to work from — maybe a phone call over a long distance in peak hours would be too expensive for you — then, in general, it's best to:

- approach a book publisher by letter, enclosing a synopsis;
- send the complete ms of a short story;
- send the complete ms of an article of less than 1,500 words;
- send a letter of enquiry about an article of more than 1,500 words.

(See also Chapter 6 for details of how to market non-fiction books, and Chapter 5 for letters of enquiry about articles.)

## One professional to another
Every detail of your first approach should be designed to give the editor a positive impression of your professionalism. Here's how to do that:

1.   DO enclose a **covering letter**. You want to establish contact with the editor, without appearing either pushy or distant. Your covering letter acts as an introductory handshake. Covering letters and letters of enquiry should be typed as normal business letters, single spaced, not double spaced like mss.

---

```
                                          Mervyn Fullohope
                                          5 Colophon Cottages
                                          Upper Case
                                          Brighton

      16th December 1988

      Rosie Burston
      Fiction Editor
      Woman
      King's Reach Tower
      Stamford Street
      London SE1 9LS


      Dear Rosie Burston

      Will you please consider the enclosed short story for
      publication in Woman at your usual rates?

      The story, 'And the Stars were Shining', is about 3,000
      words long.

      I enclose the customary stamped addressed envelope.

      Yours sincerely



      Mervyn Fullohope
```

---

How to write a covering letter.

2. DO keep your letter **brief and to the point**. It shouldn't be necessary to tell the editor what your enclosed ms is all about, or to explain the point of your short story — that should all be evident from the ms itself or from your synopsis. (A letter of enquiry sent by itself, of course, needs more detail.)

3. DO find out the **name of the appropriate editor** if you possibly can. Many magazines list the various editorial functions, usually among the early pages, or you can call the company's switchboard and ask for the name you need. Failing all else, then 'Dear Editor' is acceptable — just. It's certainly better than 'To whom it may concern' or anything like that.

4. DO enclose an **SAE** big enough and bearing adequate postage for the return of the work. This is a convention that writers ignore at the risk of never hearing of their ms again. Every publishing office has at least one drawer full of unsolicited mss sent without either a return envelope or postage. The editor didn't invite them, so why do these writers expect him to stand the cost of returning them? Small magazines in particular just can't afford to pay for stationery and stamps to return unsolicited material.

**And how not to do it**
1. DON'T send a covering letter that will take the editor as long to read as your ms would, telling him the history of your life and your writing career and assuring him that your family, friends and writers' group consider you a genius.

2. DON'T embarrass the editor with emotional blackmail. His heart will sink and his hackles will rise as he reads that you're unemployed and need the money to feed your children, that you're ninety-nine and unlikely to survive beyond his next issue, or that your doctor has prescribed creative writing as therapy following your nervous breakdown and of course any suggestion of a rejection might tip you over the edge again.

3. DON'T be either grovelling, condescending or demanding — just be businesslike. Any other approach will raise doubts in the editor's mind about your professionalism, and by implication about whether you'll be reliable and reasonable to work with in the future.

4. DON'T send any piece to more than one market at a time — editors won't look kindly on a writer who acquires a reputation for doing this.

5. DON'T use umpteen-times recycled envelopes. We all like to save

6 Nether Avenue
Satchelmouth
Lincoln

Macdonald Margin
Editor in Chief
The Southeastern Articulator
London

Dear Mac

I'm enclosing a batch - ten or so - of my short stories.
I hope you'll like at least a few well enough to publish
them - and pay.

My friends think my stories are a lot better than most of
the stuff that's getting published. What do you think? By
the way, I've tried one or two other mags, but the editors
were stocked up, they said. None of the stories have been
published before, so you can have first choice.

I know I'm supposed to enclose a stamped addressed envelope,
but you don't have to send these copies back - just let me
know what you decide, one way or the other. I'd be <u>very</u>
grateful, too, if you could give me a few comments about
the stories. Any advice at all would be welcome. <u>Please</u>
don't give me the usual 'The editor regrets' brush-off.
It's so discouraging. Sometimes I think editors just don't
give a damn about a writer's feelings. I'm sure you're not
like that, Mac. A few tips on where else I could try would
be useful, too, just in case you don't use short stories at
all (I haven't actually seen your magazine - or is it a
newspaper? - but I've seen it mentioned a few times somewhere).

Anyway, thanks for your time, and all the best!

Barney Blunder, hopeful writer.

How *not* to write a covering letter.

trees, not to mention money, but keep the economy labels and impenetrable layers of Sellotape for your private letters. Economies like this in business correspondence are counter-productive. They project entirely the wrong image, that of the amateur 'scribbler'. And DON'T send an SAE so decrepit that the editor will cringe and wonder how often it's been licked before. William Brohaugh, editor of *Writer's Digest* magazine, says in his book *Professional Etiquette for Writers* that using recycled envelopes to present your ms is like 'wearing a rumpled suit to a job interview'.

6. DON'T, either, use your company's letterheaded paper, or send your ms in envelopes bearing their logo and franked at their expense. This practice has the taint of petty stinginess, and does not inspire confidence.

---

## CHECKLIST

Check these before you make your first contact with an editor:

1. You're contacting an appropriate outlet.

2. You've ascertained as far as you can that you're following the publisher's preferred method of approach.

3. You've checked on the name of the appropriate editor.

4. Your covering letter/letter of enquiry is businesslike and totally to the point.

5. You have not brought in any irrelevancies.

6. You've enclosed a suitable SAE with your story or article, or return postage with your full-length ms.

7. Your stationery is crisp and clean, as is appropriate to your professionalism.

---

**Insider tip:** Phrase your letter very carefully, and try to assess the effect your words will have on the editor who reads it. For instance, the following sentences are guaranteed to trigger editorial alarms:

● 'Here is a short story that is a good deal better than those you've been publishing lately...'

● 'I am sure you have a lot better taste than those editors who didn't appreciate this story...'

- 'I am sixteen years old, and have decided to make writing my career...'
- 'A rejection won't discourage me. It's my life's ambition to get my work published in your magazine, so I'll keep trying till I succeed...'
- 'You will appreciate that I am a beginner, which is why I'm sending my work to you before I try to get published in something more literary...'
- 'Caution: This story is copyright, and I have taken the precaution of lodging a dated copy with my solicitor...'

## HOW TO COPE WITH REJECTION

Rejection — a dismal word for a depressing event: an editor has refused your brain-child. But don't equate rejection with dejection. It happens to (almost) every writer. Hardly surprising, with hundreds of mss jostling for every opening.

The best coping strategy is to build up a regular output. Always have work in hand as well as out 'on spec'. Don't invest all your dreams in one ms. If you're writing novels, start the next one as soon as, or even before, you've sent off your ms to a publisher.

And if your ms does thud back on to your doormat, *please* don't:

- tear it up and throw it away;
- iron it and send it straight out again;
- write an indignant letter to the editor, questioning his decision, his brains and his origins;
- spread jam on his rejection slip and post it back.

### What to do
Instead, take some constructive action. Try to analyse what went wrong. Get some practice in developing your most precious asset as a writer — the ability to make an objective criticism of your own work. Ask yourself the questions in the checklist on the next page — and be honest, for if you refuse to face the truth, you're only fooling yourself.

If you've answered 'Not sure' or 'No' to *any* of these questions, then you've been less than totally professional in your approach. It doesn't pay to skimp the hard work.

### What if your answers are all 'Yes'?
Then possibly your ms has been rejected for one of the following reasons:

- However wonderful you, your best friend, or your writers' group believe it is, your work is not up to publishable standards. That means that you probably haven't researched, organised or written it well enough — or maybe it's just plain dull. Sorry to be brutal, but about 90% of unsolicited mss fail for these reasons.

● The publisher already has a stock of this kind of material. Yours

| CHECKLIST | | | |
|---|---|---|---|
| | Yes | Not sure | No |
| 1. Are you sure that the work is as good *in every way* as you could possibly make it? | | | |
| 2. Did you check the accuracy of every fact and reference? | | | |
| 3. Are you sure you sent the work to an appropriate market? | | | |
| 4. Did you check *for yourself* that your target market is currently willing to look at unsolicited mss? | | | |
| 5. Did you check *for yourself* that the slot you aimed at is not usually or exclusively written by staff or by commissioned writers? | | | |
| 6. Did you study your market thoroughly? | | | |
| 7. Did you tailor the work to suit the style, tone, language and length of your market? | | | |
| 8. Did you check your spelling, grammar, punctuation and syntax? | | | |
| 9. Did you indicate the number of words? | | | |
| 10. Did you present an ms that is clean, clear, neat, typed on plain A4 white paper, double-spaced, on one side of the paper only, with decent margins? | | | |

would have to be sensational to be bought at this time. You're out of luck with your timing — a hazard of freelancing.

- The editor has recently bought/commissioned/published something very similar. He might tell you this. The first two are simple misfortunes. The third would mean that your market research hasn't been as good as you thought.

- There's been a change of editor and/or editorial policy. That's pure bad luck — *unless* you haven't checked the market recently.

- The editor didn't like what you sent him. If he doesn't bother to tell you this, you'll never know. Another editor might love it.

## Two questions

New writers often ask:

- *'Do editors really read every ms they receive?'*

The answer to that is 'Yes'. And 'No'. Yes, they do look at every ms that comes in — no one would consciously risk missing a gem, so everything is looked at. But no, they don't read every ms right through to the end. They don't need to. An experienced editor or publisher's reader can tell from a rapid scan whether a submission is of potential value *to him*. If he doesn't think it is, he won't waste time reading it right through.

It's pointless to get up to the tricks some writers try, to catch out a 'lazy' or 'prejudiced' editor. So forget about the hair or the spot of glue between the pages. They prove nothing.

- *'Why don't editors tell me where I'm going wrong? Rejection slips are no help at all, so why don't they give me the advice I ask for?'*

It's true that very few editors offer advice to writers. Writers, especially inexperienced ones, tend to think this is unfair. However, there are good reasons:

- Lack of time is one. Depending on its scope, an editorial office might receive upwards of twenty or so mss every day. To spend even a few minutes giving constructive advice on every one would occupy a large part of an editor's working day — and it isn't his job to do that.

- As explained above, an editor doesn't need to read the whole script to know if it interests him or not. He certainly doesn't need to give the ms a thorough critical appraisal. And to try to give a critique of a piece of work based on anything less than a complete critical reading might even do more harm than good. You wouldn't be getting a fair criticism at all, only whatever the editor thought might be useful comments *based on a very quick scan*.

● An editor's job is to find material that's suitable for his publication, not to give writing tutorials. The writing is *your* job. If you send something that is *almost* right, the editor will more than likely give you a few pointers and might ask you to do a rewrite for him 'on spec'. But when you submit an unsolicited ms, you have to remember that you're offering goods for sale in a commercial market-place. If you were selling lampshades, you wouldn't ask your customers to show you how to make them, would you?

## How books are dealt with

Most book publishers employ freelance readers to read, assess and report on unsolicited mss. These readers are usually experts in their field — experienced editors, authors and academics — and it's on their recommendation that an ms is either rejected outright or passed on for further consideration by a second reader or by an in-house editorial team.

A publisher's reader has no authority to accept a book, but his decision to reject one is seldom questioned. The acceptance rate for unsolicited book mss is very low. One publisher's reader reckons that he's only seen two out of the five thousand or so books he's assessed actually get into print. (This is not the glamorous job many people think it is.)

Do keep a sense of proportion, then, if the first publisher on your list rejects your first novel. You're certainly not alone.

## Whatever you do, DON'T do this

That comment earlier about not writing in anger to complain about a rejection was not entirely a joke. A magazine editor showed a recent writers' conference a letter she had received from a young writer whose short story she had rejected. The writer had explained at length in his covering letter that this was his first attempt to get his work published. In a sympathetic gesture, trying to 'sugar the pill' a little for a beginner, the editor took the trouble to offer him a few comments (she thought constructively) about why she didn't think the story worked, and why it wasn't right for her magazine. By return of post came a letter that now smoulders in that editor's 'Horrors' file — five closely handwritten foolscap pages of abuse and outrage, attacking the editor, her magazine and everything in it, in detail, and above all condemning the 'brevity and inadequacy' of her 'insulting' rejection.

If you can't resist the temptation to let off steam, write the letter — but DON'T POST IT. Such a response is a sure way to get your name on any editor's 'writers I never want to hear from again' list.

*'...and that's for the story...and that's for the
poem...and that's for the novel...'*

The following 'rejections of rejections' are not recommended either:

- 'Please read this again. I feel sure you must have missed the whole point of the story...'
- 'It was with considerable amazement that I received my returned manuscript this morning. I would have thought that the least you could do was to tell me what you thought was wrong with it. Here is another story. Kindly let me have a swift response to this one, with full details of your reasons, should you reject this one as well...'
- 'How could you! Your rejection has cut me to the quick. I may never have the confidence to write another word...'
- 'You just don't have the guts to give an original talent a chance...'
- 'I am returning your rejection slip herewith. I regret that it is not suited to my requirements at present...'

---

**Persistence pays, though ...**

The thriller writer John Creasey earned 774 rejections before he made his first sale.

---

# 3
# Self-Financed Publishing

## IS IT FOR YOU?

You'll come across many opinions that condemn any form of self-publishing, and which hold that if what you've written is worth publishing, then somehow, somewhere, some day a publisher will recognise it as such and accept it. They cite examples of bestsellers (*The Day of the Jackal* is a favourite) that bounced in and out of a dozen publishing houses before they were spotted by a bright editor and made their authors rich and famous and drove them into tax-exile.

This does happen occasionally, but most publishers don't get it wrong as often as frustrated writers would like to believe. Many, many books are rejected because they're not remotely up to publishable standards.

As a general rule, a publisher accepts a book and finances its publication because *in his judgement* it will add to his profits or his prestige — preferably both. Publishing is a business, and a book might be rejected simply because it isn't considered to be commercially viable or because it isn't quite suitable for that particular publisher's list. If your book keeps on coming back with editorial regrets, it might be wise to abandon that one and write another, better book.

However, if you feel confident enough of your book's merit, or if you'd just like the adventure of going-it-alone, there's nothing to stop you publishing it at your own expense — and your own risk. Provided, that is, that you understand just what you're taking on.

Do take a very careful look at what's involved. If you get carried away on a cloud of 'publication at any price' euphoria, you could be in for problems.

| CHECKLIST | | |
| --- | --- | --- |
| Is self-publishing a real option for *you*? Before you commit yourself, ask yourself these questions: | Yes | No |
| 1.  Do you have the necessary capital to fund the venture at the start? Costs could be anything from £60 or so to have 100 greeting cards printed with your own poetry to upwards of £1,500 for typesetting, printing and binding a few hundred copies of a very modest book. Don't offset any projected sales against these costs — there might not be any. | | |
| 2.  Can you afford to lose this money if it all goes wrong? Be realistic, because any such venture has an inbuilt risk factor. | | |
| 3.  Do you know how to prepare the copy yourself (or are you willing to learn) so that you can give the typesetter good enough copy to work from? If not, you'll have to add these services — editing, typing, checking for errors, correcting your proofs — to the costs. | | |
| 4.  Have you identified potential sales outlets? (Don't include family and friends who swear they'll buy a copy — they'll probably expect a freebie.) Is there *really* a market for what you want to write? | | |
| 5.  Do you have the time, energy and stamina to go out and sell your product? Or can you afford the services of a freelance representative if you want to sell your product through bookshops or other commercial outlets? | | |
| If you've answered 'No' to *any* of these, perhaps you should think again. | | |

## WHAT A REPUTABLE PUBLISHER DOES FOR YOU

When a reputable commercial publisher accepts a book for publication, he will:

- enter into a legal contract with you, agreeing the terms under which he'll publish your book, and giving full details of all rights and royalties agreed;
- possibly (but not invariably) pay you a lump sum in advance against the royalties you'll eventually earn from the book;
- make all the arrangements for editing, designing, printing and binding the book;
- arrange all the advertising, promotion, sales and distribution;
- handle all the accounting work;
- bear the cost of all the above.

He'll do all these things to the best of his ability — because *his* money and *his* reputation are at stake.

You can see, then, how important it is to know what you're taking on. You won't have all this experience, expertise, organisation and finance behind you. You'll be on your own, and you'll be taking all the risks.

Still interested? Then let's get the biggest risk of all out of the way, so that at least you have a fair chance of getting what you pay for.

## BEWARE THE 'VANITY' PUBLISHER

He isn't hard to recognise. 'Authors! If you've written a book that deserves to be published, write to us...' he sings from the small ads in the national press. 'Publisher invites manuscripts...', 'Let us publish your poetry...'

What a tempting siren song it is, especially if you're smarting from yet another rejection. But...

**Reputable publishers do not advertise for manuscripts.** Why should they? They're knee-deep already. They can pick and choose. And they choose very carefully indeed, because, as you've just seen, they're risking their money and reputation on their choice.

The vanity publisher risks nothing. He gets his money up front *from you*, and he has no reputation in the business, anyway.

He'll give you *no* editorial assessment, advice or service. He'll print your work exactly as you supply it, warts and all. He'll contract to bind only a small proportion of the copies you pay for, with an arrangement to print others as orders come in.

What orders? However many review copies he sends out, you won't get any reviews. The vanity publishers' names are well known in the trade. No reputable reviewer or publication will feature their products. No bookseller will stock them.

So where does that leave you? Heavily out of pocket, disillusioned and disappointed. Probably angry. And left to do the selling yourself. There's always a risk, too, that you might not even have a book to sell.

*'A poem called A Host of Golden Daffodils, Mrs Keatsworth? Wonderful! Just the kind of modern, original work we want to publish. Just send your cheque...'*

## One author's bitter experience

Two or three years ago, writer Charles R. Wickins, who lives in the Channel Islands, sent a short novel he'd written to a publisher called New Horizon, whose advertisements he'd read. He didn't try to place the book anywhere else. New Horizon accepted it at once. Mr Wickins signed a contract which promised him 400 copies of the book for about £1,600, to be paid in three instalments. Delighted to be given the chance to 'back his own horse', he sent the first instalment. Then the second. And he waited... and waited...

He was still waiting, many months later, when an anonymous 'friend' sent him a cutting from *Private Eye* which told him he'd been duped. New Horizon's directors 'went abroad' shortly after this. Mr Wickins never saw a single copy of his book, and never recovered a penny.

## Be cautious about poetry, too

Alan Bond is an active campaigner for high standards in poetry. A well-established writer and poet (he won the 1987 Samuel Laycock Trophy in the Annual International Lancashire Dialect Society Competition), Alan has become increasingly perturbed about the activities of some publishers who advertise for poetry to publish. He decided to put one of them to the test.

Before a witness, he dashed off two 'poems' in twenty-eight seconds, and sent them off under a pseudonym.

Back came an offer to publish both poems — 'Just the kind of contemporary poems we're looking for' — in an anthology, if Alan would pay the publisher £7.50 for the publication of each poem. In return for this, he would get two copies of the anthology, one for each £7.50 paid. If he wanted more, he could have the privilege of buying them at £4.50 per copy.

Here are the spoof poems, printed here with Alan Bond's permission:

**Flying Eyes**

And then the bird
The big black
Bird
Flew toward my eyes.
I waved my arms
The bird flapped a wing.
I let it go.

**By Telecom**

He rang.
I won't be long.
I waited,
He rang again.
The buses, the taxis, the
Excuses.
The door waits open.
I wait and wait and wait.

You can draw your own conclusions about the standard of selection applied by *that* 'publisher'. Would you be proud to see *your* work published alongside rubbish like that?

### Don't risk your reputation

If you want to build up a reputation as a poet, steer well clear of paying to get your poetry published in an anthology of this kind. No matter how good *your* poems might be, you'll have no control over the selection of the other poems in the anthology. Your reputation could be badly tarnished, perhaps irretrievably.

Don't fall for these seductive advertisements. The risks are far too great.

## YOUR SELF-PUBLISHING OPTIONS

### Inexpensive methods

1. You could do the whole thing yourself, with a **typewriter** and access to a **photocopier** or **duplicating** machine.

2. You could produce it on a **word processor** or **computer**. If this is an option for you, read *The Wordsmith* magazine — it could be just what you need.

3. You could have the text set and printed by your **local 'instant print' shop**, and collate the pages yourself. Or there might be a **community press** in your district, with simple printing equipment. Enquire at the library.

There's an inexpensive and excellent manual on basic printing and production, *Print — how you can do it yourself*, by Jonathan Zeitlyn (now in its fourth edition). This tells you everything you need to know about putting your work into print, and includes a vast amount of information about paper suppliers, printers, books on the subject and so on.

**Poetry booklets**

Joan B. Howes has had many poems published in magazines. She also publishes her own poetry in **booklets** which she sells as fund raisers, mainly for Animal Rescue. Her 1987 booklet *Orange and Sauce* has ten poems attractively printed on card. It cost Joan £75 for 100 copies, which she sold at a small profit through local bookshops. She sent a copy to her local paper, and it was well reviewed which helped to sell it.

Besides raising a little money for a good cause, Joan finds the booklets make very acceptable small gifts, and provide a 'shop window' for her poetry.

**Greeting cards**

You can have your poetry or short pieces of prose printed up in greeting cards for Christmas and other occasions. The **Afton Press** in Carnoustie, Scotland, specialises in this. The cost depends very much on the number of cards you order, but a rough guide would be about £30 for fifty cards, with the cost dropping rapidly for larger quantities down to about £55 for 300 cards. Penny Glenday will send you details of prices of this and other Afton printing services on request.

**PUBLISHING YOUR OWN BOOK**

There are several good books available to guide you with an ambitious venture like this. Going it alone can be well worth all the effort. Harry Mulholland has certainly found this to be so, with his series of mountain guidebooks.

> Self-publishing opens up exciting prospects of promoting projects
> in which you believe, with complete control of their design and
> content. Also production time is counted in months, not a year or
> more. To the usual 10% royalty you add the publisher's profit and
> the postman can become your friend bringing orders or cheques —
> not rejected manuscripts.
>
> Harry Mulholland.

Harry has put all his own know-how and experience into his highly
regarded book *Guide to Self-publishing — The A–Z of Getting Yourself
into Print*. The book is self-published (of course), and you can get it
through bookshops or direct from Harry's own publishing company
Mulholland-Wirral at £5.95 plus 75p post and packing. The address is
in the appendices.

### It could be a bestseller...
After Aeron Clement's badger saga *The Cold Moons* had been rejected
by two major publishers, his friend Bernard Kindred, landlord of his
local pub, suggested they should publish the book themselves. The rest
is publishing history.

Just two weeks after publication, they had sold more than a thousand
copies at £10.95 each, more than recouping their £10,000 investment. By
March 1988 it was in the hardback bestseller lists, and Penguin had paid
£140,000 for the paperback rights.

*The Cold Moons*, published by Kindredson Publishing Ltd, will
almost certainly make Aeron Clement a millionaire.

### Recommended books
● *Guide to Self-Publishing — The A–Z of Getting Yourself into Print*
  by Harry Mulholland — see above.

● *How to Publish Yourself* and *How to Publish Your Poetry*, both
  by Peter Finch. Here is practical guidance on every aspect of self-
  publishing, from your first decision to take the plunge to how to
  market your product.

● *Magazine and Journal Production* by Michael Barnard. Not a
  'how to do it' book, but an introduction to all the techniques
  and processes involved. There's a comprehensive twenty-four page
  glossary, but, oddly, no index.

- *Copy Prep* by Jill Baker. How to edit and prepare copy for typesetting, how to read proofs and so on, including a useful chapter on finding and using freelance services.

- *Editing for Print* by Geoffrey Rogers. A guide to the business and technicalities of publishing, including descriptions of the various editorial functions, book and magazine production methods, scheduling, budgeting, printing processes and a good deal more.

- *Marketing for Small Publishers* by Keith Smith tells you how to promote your book, to the public and to the trade, how to cost, design and write a media campaign, how to sell it and where, and how to arrange distribution.

- *The Craft of Copywriting* and *Do Your Own Advertising*, both by Alastair Crompton, deal with the skills and techniques of promoting and selling just about everything (as well as being an eye-opening read about the advertising industry). These two books have a special interest for the aspiring self-publisher because they were both originally published by Alastair Crompton himself, in very handsome hardbacks which sold well (the hardback editions are almost out of print now). They were so attractive and successful, in fact, that Century Hutchinson bought the paperback rights in 1986, and it's these paperback editions that you can buy now.

### Associations
There's an **Association of Little Presses**, which you can join to benefit from its members' advice and experience — see **Associations and Societies Open to Unpublished Writers** on page 152.

### Scriptmate — a comprehensive, high-powered service
If you're willing (and able) to invest a fairly substantial amount of money in your project, you can have the whole lot done for you, by **Scriptmate**.

In 1986 Ann Kritzinger won a top prize in a contest sponsored by the London Enterprise Agency, City accountants Ernst and Whinney, and the London *Standard*. Ann's scheme was for a high-tech/low-cost printing service, based on laser printing, to enable authors to publish short-run paperbacks themselves, and to allow publishers to produce short runs of books for market-testing purposes.

Ann was already running her successful editorial advisory service, Scriptmate, and the award meant that she could afford to extend into the field of high-tech printing.

The costing system is complex, because every customer's needs are different, and there's a reduced rate for copy supplied on disk, but as a rough guide, a 120 page book, text supplied in manuscript form, would cost somewhere between £1,300 and £1,400 for 500 copies. This is for setting, printing and binding — editorial services are charged separately. There is provision for re-ordering at short notice, and for converting your book to a much cheaper system suitable for longer runs, should you find yourself with a bestseller on your hands.

Ann Kritzinger will send you full details of all the Scriptmate Services, including their ms criticism service, on request.

### For writers of academic material
**Deanhouse Limited** is a small academic publisher specialising in educational books, academic monographs, occasional papers and academic journals. Deanhouse offers a full editorial and publishing service for individual authors, societies, associations and organisations. The service is also available to overseas authors who want to be published under a UK imprint.

For full details of publishing terms, costs and so on, contact Roland P. Seymour, Deanhouse Limited — *see* **Printing/publishing services** on page 162. (Please note: Deanhouse handles academic material *only*.)

### Required by law
You are legally required to send one copy of your publication to the **British Library Copyright Receipt Office**, where every publication produced in the UK must be lodged.

Then you'll eventually receive a demand from the **Agent for the Libraries**, Mr A. T. Smail, for a further five copies for distribution to the **copyright libraries** (Oxford, Cambridge, Dublin, Scotland and Wales). You won't get any payment for these six copies, but don't begrudge them too much. For one thing, their deposit with the libraries ensures that there is an official record of their existence, which might be useful in the event of any copyright problem, and for another, it's to these libraries' lists that other libraries throughout the English-speaking world look for potential additions to their own lists.

# 4
# Writing Competitions

Cash prizes, publication, prestige, possibly fame — they're all on offer in the hundreds of writing competitions organised every year. Enter as many as you can. You never know what you can do...

Paul Heapy read about a science fiction short-story competition being run by *The Sunday Times* jointly with publishers Victor Gollancz, who have been building up a strong science fiction list over the last few years. Intrigued by what he read, he decided to enter.

> They did the work for me. Had it been simply an SF story competition, no doubt I would not have entered. After all, I thought of myself as a poet. But J. G. Ballard wrote a superb introductory piece setting out his conception of what SF should be for. And great soul that he is, I could only agree. So when I won, it was just as though they had reached out and tapped me on the shoulder.
>
> Paul Heapy.

Paul won first prize, his story was published, and Gollancz invited him to write a science fiction novel. He had never written *any kind* of short story before.

## WHAT COULD YOU WIN?

Publication is the most sought-after prize of all. Competitions that guarantee publication of the winning entries attract by far the biggest postbags.

Most prizes are quite modest: a book token or a trophy, or a cash prize that will at least help fund your writing — most cash prizes are between £25 and several hundred pounds.

But you *might* win a spectacular sum, like the £5,000 first prize in the Arvon Foundation Biennial Poetry Competition. There are also prizes on offer for *unpublished* novels, for instance the Betty Trask Awards for a romantic first novel by a writer under 35, which is worth a total of £17,500, and the Georgette Heyer Historical Novel Prize (£5,000 in prize-money) both with guaranteed publication.

### Have a go at the big ones

Don't be put off entering big competitions by the thought of all the famous writers you might be up against. Entries are often judged on a 'no name on the entry' basis, especially big poetry competitions. The judges don't know who wrote what till the adjudication is complete. There are several ways of organising this, and each competition carries details of its preferred method in its literature and entry forms.

In practice, however, a very big competition is more a gamble than a contest. The usual procedure is that the entries are divided up among a panel of adjudicators, each of whom chooses what he considers to be the best entries from his batch. Then all the judges read all the short-listed manuscripts *only*, so if a judge eliminates your entry in the first round, no one else will see it. From the short-list, each judge selects his potential winners, and from these survivors the eventual winners are chosen — sometimes with a good deal of heat. Philip Larkin once said in public that the poem his three fellow-judges of a major poetry competition had selected as the overall winner didn't make good sense.

## WHAT DO THE JUDGES LOOK FOR?

In **short-story competitions**, the same qualities an editor looks for:

- a story that grabs and holds the reader's interest;
- a story that stimulates the desire to know 'what happens next';
- a story that is soundly structured;
- a story that is fluently written.

Note, *a story*. One of the most common faults judges find is that many writers don't really understand what a short story is and what it is not — see Chapter 8.

In **poetry**, the qualities an adjudicator looks for were summarised by the late Howard Sergeant MBE, who was founding editor of *Outposts Poetry Quarterly* for over 40 years. Howard's criteria are reproduced here by kind permission of his widow, Jean. They are:

- craftsmanship;

- adequate command of the tone and language appropriate to the poem in question;
- individual vision and use of imagination;
- genuine feeling and personal contact.

In **plays** the criteria sought by judges vary enormously because of the differences in the facilities and economics of the companies that organise them. Each competition will give some indication of its requirements in its literature, and it will be an advantage to make yourself familiar with the venue where the winning plays might eventually be performed, so that you can avoid obviously impossible special effects and staging.

## ENTERING WRITING COMPETITIONS

### The DOs

1.  DO **read the rules**. That's obvious, you say? You would be very surprised to see how many people don't bother. Yet it's pretty foolish to risk instant elimination in this way. If you infringe *any* of the rules, you're out — and no one will send back your entry fee.
2.  DO **respect the set word or line limits**. The judges *will* notice if you don't, because they are bound by the rules, too. They won't risk the wrath of other competitors by awarding a prize to a piece that's either too long or too short according to the rules.
3.  DO **write what is asked for**. Some writers don't seem to realise that, for instance, an article sent to a short-story competition will be thrown out at once. They're wasting their time and their entry fees.
4.  DO **study your 'market'**. If the prize includes publication, it makes sense to study at least one or two issues of the magazine or newspaper that will print the winners, so you can be sure your entry is appropriate. Publication in a national women's or 'family' magazine, for example, would rule out explicit sex and violence, or over-strong language.
5.  DO **keep a copy** of your entry, whether or not the original will be returned (and most competitions don't return entries).
6.  DO **stick to the standard ms layouts**, unless the rules say otherwise.
7.  DO **remember that judges**, like editors, **are human** (yes, truly), and could be put off by a badly presented entry.

### And the DON'Ts

1.  DON'T be tempted to enter any competition that requires you to **give up your copyright**. However attractive the prizes, you could be

signing away your rights to long-term benefits. Your poem might become a favourite for anthologies or even school textbooks, your short story might be adapted for radio or TV — it might even be the basis of a series — and you would have no claim at all to *any* payment.

2. DON'T **wrap your entry up in elaborate packaging**. Fancy folders, decorated cover-sheets, ribbon bows and suchlike are just a nuisance to the organisers, and will go straight into the waste bucket. One organiser remarked that she had received a Jiffy-bag containing a cardboard document wallet inside which was a mass of tissue paper covering a plastic sleeve, all to protect a single poem. It's odd, too, how the fanciest packaging, according to adjudicators' reports, almost invariably contains the worst entries.

3. DON'T **forget to enclose your entry fee**. Your entry will be disqualified without it, and it's most unlikely that the organisers will send you a reminder.

4. DON'T **be too devastated if you don't win**. Remember that all competitions are a lottery to some extent. Just keep trying. It's wonderful practice in writing to set lengths about set subjects — and remember Paul Heapy.

---

### CHECKLIST

Check these points before sending off a competition entry:

1. Have you read *all* the rules?

2. Is your entry appropriate to the competition subject?

3. Is your entry suitable for publication (if applicable)?

4. Is it within the stipulated lengths?

5. Have you typed it in the standard layout?

6. On white A4 paper?

7. Have you kept a copy?

8. Have you understood and followed any special instructions about anonymous entry and so on?

9. Have you enclosed the correct entry fee, and made your cheque or postal order payable to the designated name?

10. Have you enclosed an SAE if one was requested?

## WHERE TO FIND OUT MORE

- Writers' circles and literary groups receive regular information.
- Your local library might have leaflets — ask at the desk if these are not displayed — some organisers ask that their leaflets should be kept for those interested enough to enquire, rather than left out to be used as shopping-list scrap-paper by browsers.
- Writers' magazines, like *Success, Writing, Writer's Monthly*, and *Freelance Market News*, list current and forthcoming competitions.
- The *Friends of Arvon Newsletter* has a competitions column.
- The *Writers' & Artists' Yearbook* and *The Writer's Handbook* list major literary awards.
- The Book Trust Information Service.
- Flyers distributed by most small literary and poetry magazines.
- National newspapers and magazines carry notices of major competitions, and some even run their own. The *Woman's Own* Short Story Competition is now an established annual event.

# 5
# Writing for Magazines and Newspapers

## WRITING ARTICLES

Take a look at your newsagent's shelves. Did you realise that nearly all the publications you see there buy most of their articles from freelance writers?

The constant demand for good articles makes them one of the easiest types of writing to sell. 'Easier to sell', however, doesn't mean easier to write. The demand is high, certainly, but the standard expected is also high.

### Potential outlets

There are literally thousands of potential outlets for articles. The *Writers' & Artists' Yearbook* lists over 600 UK newspapers and magazines that publish (and pay for) articles. *Willing's Press Guide* lists more than 10,000 UK publications, including trade, professional and specialist magazines, and many of these welcome freelance contributions relevant to their subject area. The *A–Z of Britain's Free Newspapers and Magazines* (published by The Association of Free Newspapers) lists about 1,000 titles.

*Freelance Market News* and the Bureau of Freelance Photographers' *Market Newsletter* are good sources of information about current markets for articles.

To write and sell freelance articles, you need:

● the ability to write clear, concise English;
● an observant eye;
● an enquiring mind;
● a professional approach to writing up your material.

> To succeed at article writing, you must study a market regularly — editors' needs change — and slant your writing to meet that requirement. Start off with a good strong 'hook' and try to end strongly too. For a saleable writing style, keep words, sentences and paragraphs short and simple. And keep on writing.
>
> Gordon Wells.

## A MANY-SPLENDOURED MEDIUM

Never mind how new you are to writing, there's sure to be at least one facet of article-writing that could give you your first taste of publication. Look at the choice:

- factual articles
- personal experiences
- human interest stories
- opinion pieces
- 'how-to' and DIY articles
- 'round-up' articles (where a number of people contribute ideas/ experiences/opinions)
- self-help and self-improvement
- interviews
- profiles
- travel features
- short-short articles and fillers

and you'll probably add more as you explore the possibilities.

### Make it shapely

Whatever your subject, an article needs to be structured into a logical and satisfying form. Like a good story, it needs a beginning, a middle and an end, but unlike a story, where you can take liberties with that order of things, an article works best with the most straightforward sequence:

1. **A strong opening paragraph**. If you've dug up some amazing or little-known fact, or if you have a strong statement to make, put it here. For example, you might open an article on *Writing as a Second Career* with: 'Mrs Thatcher's Home Secretary, Douglas Hurd, spends his spare time writing political thrillers — and he gets them published. How many other famous people have a writing career as a second string?'

It's quite a common misjudgement for beginners to save their juiciest fact till the end. But if you don't grab the reader's attention right away, he might not bother to read to the end, so your amazing discovery is lost anyway. Feed him the tastiest titbit first, and save the second-best to the last.

2. **The middle**, the main course. This should be packed with interesting information written in the most logical sequence, but not simply given as a list of facts. Spice it with anecdotes, questions, opinions.

3. **The closing paragraph.** This should provide a satisfying rounding-off, summarising in some way what you've been saying. It's a good idea to refer back, however obliquely, to your first paragraph: 'Given the chance, would Douglas Hurd give up politics to write full-time?' Or give your reader a question of his own to consider: 'Would *you* give up your day-job to risk writing as a career?' If you do have another interesting fact to offer, you could conclude with that: 'Agatha Christie's main career was writing. So was her second string. She wrote six romantic-psychological novels under the pen-name of Mary Westmacott. These novels, as she wrote in her *Autobiography*, were the only ones that really satisfied her. Her crime novels were her bread and butter.'

## Shorts and short-shorts

The terms 'short articles' and 'short-short' articles sometimes puzzle new writers. They don't really have any strict definitions. What would be considered a short article by one magazine might be a full-length feature to another. Generally speaking, however, you can work on the basis that:

- a **short-short article** is 200–500 words;
- a **short article** is 500–750 words;
- an **article** is usually 750–2,000 words.

You should always check the length preferences of any particular market, as a matter of course, before you send them any material.

## Fillers

A **filler** is a short item fitted into a small space so that a page won't be left with blank spaces where the main items are not long enough to fill it.

Anecdotes, humorous verse, puzzles, jokes, cartoons, tips and hints, press errors, odd facts, brain-teasers, quotations — all these are used as fillers, and many magazines buy them from freelances.

Keep an eye open for likely filler slots, and collect odd pieces of information, jokes and suchlike that fall your way. You might be able to make use of them.

## Readers' letters

These, too, come into the category of fillers, but they've acquired a status of their own and are now a strong selling feature for many publications.

Payment can be quite high, as much as the £30 paid by *Weekend* for their weekly 'star' letter. The average payment is around £5 or £6, and some magazines 'pay' in prizes instead of cash.

'Letters to the editor' are a popular starting point for many new writers. Don't be misled into thinking that because they're short they're easy to write and sell. A successful letter has probably been worked on just as carefully as any article — it has to be tailored to its market, too.

Every publication has its own style. You should look at points like:

● Does the publication prefer long or short letters?
● Is the tone of the letters neutral? cosy? argumentative? cynical? amused? helpful? sympathetic? belligerent?
● Do any of the letters raise controversial issues?
● Are any of the letters obvious responses to correspondence or features that appeared in previous issues of the magazine?

Readers' letters are **very good practice** for an aspiring article-writer because they demand the same kind of disciplines: no waffle, no wordiness, and the letter must make its point as clearly and concisely as possible.

You can use pen-names if you like. Editors might not want to see the same names appearing too often in their letters pages. (An exception to this seems to be a man called Max Nottingham, whose name crops up with astonishing regularity in newspapers, magazines and programmes like Radio Four's 'PM', in which listeners' letters are read out. He seems to be a one-man letter-writing industry. It would be interesting to know if he writes under other names, too.)

## No SAE required

'Readers' letters' is one area where the normal convention of enclosing an SAE doesn't apply. Letters are never returned and are only acknowledged if they're used. Voucher copies are not sent. You might receive advance notice that your letter will be printed, or you might hear nothing till you get your payment.

## WHAT WILL YOU WRITE YOUR ARTICLE ABOUT?

Your best bet if you're a beginner is to write about something you know well. The better you know your subject the more confidently you'll handle it, and your confidence will communicate itself to your reader. And don't forget that the first reader who will see your article is an editor. An experienced editor can sense at once if a writer is trying to tackle a subject he isn't really comfortable with.

Your knowledge of the subject will probably already have given you some knowledge of the publications that might be interested in printing your articles. You'll need that knowledge, because without doubt you'll be able to write more than one article on your subject, each slanted to a different market.

For instance, if your hobby is collecting old gramophone records, you could write about

- where to find them
- how to store them
- how much they cost
- the equipment needed to play them
- the artists who made them

...and much, much more, as the subject diagram on page 78 shows.

Try making your own subject diagram. Write down the main subject in the middle of a (large) sheet of paper, and write its main branches all round it. You'll quickly see how the branches begin to shoot out sub-branches, and probably even the sub-branches could produce twigs. This kind of lateral thinking is a lot more productive than simply making a linear list. It's a very powerful brainstormer.

### What do you know already?
You can use the same exercise to draft out your knowledge of sources of information on your subject, and on possible markets. You'll find the ideas coming almost faster than you can write them down.

### Make it convincing
Whatever your subject, you should make it your business to gather enough information and solid facts about it to write a convincing, fact-packed article. The editorial nose will quickly sniff out a 'scissors-and-paste' job — that is, a piece cobbled together from reference books and other people's opinions. That doesn't mean, of course, that you can't make use of other people's findings and conclusions (provided you don't infringe their copyright), but your article will

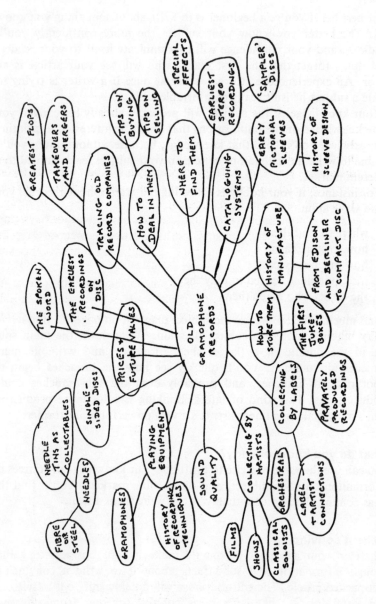

How to make a subject diagram.

be stillborn if it contains little or nothing of your own thoughts and feelings.

You'll often find, too, that it will take several rewrites to achieve a convincingly 'spontaneous' style. Don't be afraid to let your own personality show through.

## Be methodical

You'll save yourself a lot of irritation, time and trouble, if you devise a simple system for filing your article and filler information as you gather it. It's infuriating if you're stuck for one small piece of information and you can't remember where you put it.

You need to be able to retrieve the information you need, quickly and easily, the minute you want it. This is especially important if you're trying to fit your writing into precious spare time sandwiched between your day job and keeping the weeds under control.

You can use document wallets, large envelopes, card index systems, or, of course, electronic storage if you have a word processor or computer. The system itself doesn't matter — what *does* matter is that you have one.

But don't let the research take over your writing time too much. As Gordon Wells says in *The Craft of Writing Articles:* 'You need to be able to find facts quickly and easily. But your hobby is writing — make sure that it does not become "fact-filing".'

*'And that's only the rejection slips.'*

### Where to look for information

- **Your local library.** If you tell the library staff what you're looking for and why you want it, you'll find them very helpful.
- *Research for Writers* by Ann Hoffmann is an indispensable source of information about how and where to find information.
- **Newspaper cuttings.** Mrs Pat Kenderdine runs a postal service — see **Information services and sources** on page 159.
- **Specialist book dealers.** There might be one locally — look in the Yellow Pages or ask at the library. There are many listed in the *Book and Magazine Collector* magazine. Or contact Jubilee Books — *see* **Information services and sources** on page 159.
- **The British Library Newspaper Library** at Colindale, North London, houses London newspapers from 1801, and English provincial, Scottish, Irish, Commonwealth and foreign newspapers from 1700. You need to apply to the Library for a reader's pass.

## HOW TO SELL YOUR ARTICLES

It's becoming more usual now to send a **query letter** before you submit an article. This has long been the accepted practice in the US, and most American editors insist on a preliminary query. Material that comes in 'over the transom' is now discouraged.

In general here in the UK, though, it's still all right to send a **short article** — up to about 1,500 words — as a complete ms. It would take an editor nearly as long to read a query letter as it does to scan a short piece. You won't get a firm acceptance on the strength of a query anyway, unless the editor knows your work already, so you might as well let him see what you can do. If he prefers a preliminary query, he'll let you know when he gives you a decision on your submission.

**Longer pieces** are another matter. It's better to query the editor first, not only to save postage and stationery costs, but also because if he does express an interest, he might have some suggestions to make about your treatment of the subject, perhaps preferring that you take a different approach or that you make it shorter than you suggested and so on.

### How to write a query letter
Your query should tell the editor three things:
1. What the **subject** of the article will be, and what angle you intend to treat it from. Use the 'bullet' system to list your points briefly and clearly. Include an indication of the proposed length.

2. Why you think his **readers would be interested** in what you have to say.

3. Why *you* are **able and qualified** to write it. If you have special qualifications — practical experience, a degree in the subject, or something like that — then include them here, but avoid dragging in qualifications, however impressive, that are totally irrelevant to the subject you'll be writing about. If you want to offer an article on, say, collecting Commonwealth commemorative stamps, your target editor is unlikely to rush off an acceptance letter because you've told him you've been practising yoga and transcendental meditation for twenty years.

Suppose you want to offer the editor of *Annabel* an article on collecting ephemera, those throw-away bits of social history: postcards, programmes, tickets, bookmarks and the like.

First, check that you have a note of the current editor's name, correctly spelled. Then structure your query something like the letter on page 82.

## BOOKS ABOUT WRITING ARTICLES

- Lisa Collier Cool, *How To Sell Every Magazine Article You Write.* An American book on the techniques of selling by query letter before you write the article. Some writers swear by this method, and some editors prefer it, but others say it's a waste of time, preferring to see the finished article. You'll have to find out for yourself if it works for you.

- Fay Goldie, *Successful Freelance Journalism.* Practical advice on writing and selling all kinds of articles from fillers to features, and tips on developing a freelance career.

- Brendan Hennessy, *Essential Feature Writing.* A practical guide to writing feature articles — how to gather, organise and target information. Forward-looking and comprehensive in its coverage.

- John Hines, *The Way to Write Magazine Articles.* Covers researching, writing and selling. Good on developing ideas.

- Raymond Hull, *How to Write 'How-To' Books and Articles.* Good American book showing in detail how to communicate your knowledge to readers. Covers collaborating, research, illustrations and promotion.

- Paul Kerton, *The Freelance Writer's Handbook.* Covers a lot of

Emily Hoarder
White Elephants
Overflow Lane
Fillingham

10th January 1989

David McColl
Editor
Annabel
D C Thomson & Co Ltd
185 Fleet Street
London EC4A 2HS

Dear Mr McColl

I am writing to enquire whether you would be interested in seeing an article about collecting ephemera.

There's plenty of scope for building up an interesting and potentially valuable collection, without too great a financial outlay. Many of your readers might be unaware of how collectable these scraps of social history have become. Some readers might not even know that such a field of collecting exists.

To begin a collection they would need to know:

* what the term 'ephemera' means: essentially items of no intrinsic value, such as postcards, cigarette cards, book-marks, tickets, magazines and newspapers, advertising material, pamphlets and so on;

* where to look for collectable items: antique and collectors' fairs, where a few dealers specialise in ephemera, jumble sales, charity shops, the attics and cellars of friends and relations...;

* approximate prices they might expect to pay;

* where there is most potential for value increases;

* the best ways to store and/or display their collection.

Once a new collector begins to realise how wide the range is, he or she often moves on to specialisation, and is soon hooked on the hobby. It's fun, it's fascinating, and it's relatively cheap.

I have been collecting ephemera myself for several years, and have recently begun to specialise in bookmarks, their design and history, and their value to the companies that issued them (they were widely used as an advertising medium).

I can supply a variety of photographs, if you wish.

The text as I plan it would be 1,750-2,000 words. I enclose a stamped addressed envelope for your reply.

Yours sincerely

(Mrs) Emily Hoarder

ground, with useful sections on article-writing and journalism, pepped up by personal contributions from well-known writers. Treat the references in this book with some caution — some of them are inaccurate.

- Gordon Wells, *The Craft of Writing Articles*. Thoroughly practical, easy to understand and full of examples and advice on writing and selling. One of the best books on this subject.

- Gordon Wells, *The Magazine Writer's Handbook*. Lists specific magazine markets, giving editorial requirements, payment rates, how to approach the editor and so on. Useful as a guide, but make sure you only use the latest edition. This is ephemeral information, more suited to a periodical than a book, because it goes out of date very quickly.

## JOURNALISM

A successful journalist is a writer who knows how to:

- tell his story within tightly focused limitations
- see his story from his reader's angle
- avoid verbosity and cut out padding
- express his meaning in clear, concise and unambiguous language
- produce quality work under pressure, to meet tight deadlines.

Robbie Gray is former chief sub-editor/night-editor of the *Daily Mirror, Daily Express, Sunday People* and *The Star*, and now works as an executive with the *West Lancashire Evening Gazette*. Asked what advice he would offer to aspiring journalists, Robbie said:

I have only to repeat the advice of Sir Hugh Cudlipp when he was editor of the *Daily Mirror:* 'Keep it simple.'

It was also Cudlipp who said: 'Never talk down to your reader.' It took me some time in my salad days to work out precisely what he meant — and, of course, it was exactly that. Never try to give the readers the impression that you think you are cleverer than they are. Never deliberately try to send them scurrying off in search of a dictionary. They don't have time, and probably won't bother.

Robbie Gray.

Most newspapers, like most magazines, buy material from freelance writers. There are three main types of newspaper: national, regional and local. The *Writers' & Artists' Yearbook* lists the nationals and a few of the regionals, but *The Writer's Handbook* gives a lot more information, listing all the major national and regional titles, with editorial names and requirements, tips about approaching them, and what they pay.

## The financial rewards

Payment varies a good deal. Some papers pay NUJ (National Union of Journalists) rates whether you're a union member or not. Others pay 'by arrangement', in which case you'll be offered what the editor thinks the piece is worth, or possibly, if he's never heard of you, what he thinks you'll be prepared to settle for. This is one of the areas where a thoroughly professional approach can really pay off. Don't invite the editor to offer you less than he might have done because your badly presented and carelessly spelled mss and your tatty recycled envelopes leave him in no doubt that he's dealing with someone who doesn't know the business.

Unless you're already a member of the NUJ, there's little use in arguing about the offer. You can either refuse it and try your luck elsewhere or you can accept it philosophically, so that you can add another item to your portfolio of published work. A strong portfolio will eventually put you in a position to negotiate fees.

NUJ rates go up to about £250 per thousand words for top-paying papers and magazines, the national press generally pays about £175 per thousand words, and there's a minimum rate of £6.80 per hundred words for the regional and local press.

## Getting your foot in the door

Local papers are your best bet to begin with. They always want:

● news stories, short and to the point, to cover local events: 'Her Majesty unveils memorial plaque', 'Local grandmother's surprise triplets';

● social issue articles: 'Save our swimming baths', 'Do our citizens want clean streets?';

● striking photographs of local people, places and events.

(Note the strong 'local' emphasis.)

## The five 'W's

When you're writing your article, make sure you haven't omitted any essential information. Check the content against the journalist's creed, the five 'W's:

● Who?

- What?
- Where?
- When?
- Why?

And if it's appropriate, add an 'H' — How?

Whether they're distributed free or not, these papers live on their advertising revenue, so short pieces stand a better chance of acceptance because they leave more room for ads.

Include a photograph or two with your article if you can. Check with the paper about preferred sizes.

Find out, too, about deadlines — this week's hot news is next week's rejection.

You'll usually be paid after publication, at some set date, and you might be expected to submit an **invoice**. Clarify this beforehand. An invoice is a simple business document, a bill asking for payment of money which is due to you. It's easy to prepare. Just make sure you include all the necessary information, as in the example.

```
                              Invoice

(999) 34123                               Oliver Columnist
                                          12 Gossip Alley
                                          Tiny Tiles
                                          By Eastborough

22nd July 1988

Basil Bond
Editor
Eastborough Tattle
Eastborough

To writing one short feature, 'Scandal
    at the Vicarage', published in
    Eastborough Tattle 15.7.88.               £25.00
```

Example of an invoice.

Articles have to be straightforward and to the point — there is little room for picturesque speech. Most important of all, facts should be absolutely accurate. Dates should be given where applicable, since while it may be obvious to you that last Sunday means last Sunday, in the chaos of an editor's office such things cannot be taken for granted. Dated material gets first priority, and in any case, it is professional procedure. If I ever quote anyone then I usually enclose a separate sheet giving details of how they can be contacted, and then the editor can verify or expand an interview, or perhaps arrange a photograph.

Give names and dates in full. There should be no reason for the editor to think you haven't done your job properly.

Writing factual pieces imposes its own discipline on the writer, and this is particularly healthy for those writers who are just starting off.

Graham Thomas.

You're never too young to start writing for publication. Graham Thomas started at 15, and was soon selling regularly to his local papers. He's now at university studying English and Philosophy, and hopes to make writing his full-time career.

### Is there a gap in the coverage?
If you spot an opening for a topic your paper isn't already covering, you could suggest ideas, perhaps for:

- a book, film or TV column
- a poetry corner
- a children's page
- any original series that *you* could supply on a regular basis.

But don't suggest any kind of competition unless you're willing to handle the entries yourself. The staff won't welcome the extra work.

## DIRECTORY OF FREE NEWSPAPERS AND MAGAZINES

The Association of Free Newspapers and Magazines (AFN) publishes an annual directory, the *A–Z of Britain's Free Newspapers and Magazines,* which lists thousands of titles, with their addresses and phone numbers, distribution areas, circulation breakdowns, advertising revenue, social status of their readership and so on. The directory costs about £30 and you can buy it from AFN, but it's sent out free to advertising agency personnel, so if you have a friend in advertising, perhaps he would let you consult his copy.

## JOURNALISM FOR DISABLED PEOPLE

Physical handicap needn't be a barrier to a successful writing career. Anyone who doubts that need only look at the achievements of Christy Nolan, overall winner of the 1987 Whitbread Awards.

> We all go to our Maker taking with us a host of untapped talents and for you this may be writing. You never know whether you can write until you try. Because it is a home-based activity which can be followed at any time of the day, writing is a good occupation for disabled people, particularly wheelchair riders. It widens social horizons and uses much of the time of which handicapped people have plenty. You are not disabled to your readers, and you compete on even terms with able-bodied writers.
>
> Pat Saunders.

Pat Saunders averages 60,000 words of published material a year. He is confined to a wheelchair and unable to hold a pen. Currently he is Assistant Editor of *Caring for Handicaps* magazine, and Director of Hampshire Disablement Information and Advice Line.

When Pat began writing a weekly column for disabled people in the *Portsmouth News*, he was surprised to find that this was the first regular feature of its kind in the country. Convinced of the widespread need for such features, he produced *All Write Now*, a booklet of practical advice and encouragement for disabled people who want to write, particularly those who want to communicate the kind of news and information that would benefit other disabled people. You can order a copy by post — *see* the reference in **Useful booklets** on page 180.

## JOURNALISM AS A CAREER

Many newspaper companies offer training in newspaper journalism and photography. The training schemes are administered by the National Council for the Training of Journalists (NCTJ). NCTJ trainees are eligible to join the NUJ.

The minimum requirements for direct employment by a newspaper as a trainee reporter are (and each category must include English):

● five subject passes in Grades A, B or C at GCE 'O'level or GCSE, or

- one 'A' level plus four 'O' levels in different subjects, or
- two 'A' levels plus two 'O' levels in different subjects.

There's no age limit to application for employment in the newspaper industry, although most new entrants are school-leavers or university graduates.

You can get information about the courses direct from NCTJ, or from The Newspaper Society. The Newspaper Society also publishes a useful booklet, *The Making of a Newspaper*, which costs 40 pence. (The training scheme details are sent free of charge.)

If you're considering journalism as a career, you'll find Peter Medina's book *Careers in Journalism* (3rd edition) very helpful. It covers all journalistic fields including radio and TV: courses, training schemes, grants and so on, illustrated with case studies.

## Other recommended books
- Liz Taylor, *The Writing Business*
- Fay Goldie, *Successful Freelance Journalism*
- Ian Linton, *Writing for a Living*
- Paul Kerton, *The Freelance Writer's Handbook*

# 6
# Writing a Non-fiction Book

Are you an expert on a subject that would interest a large number of people? Do you have first-hand experience or knowledge that might benefit, profit, intrigue, amuse or inspire others? Have you set up and run a successful business? Built your own house? Prospected for gold in the Andes? Perhaps then you've already thought of writing a book about it, but didn't know where to begin.

## IS YOUR IDEA FEASIBLE?

Before you commit yourself to the project and all the hard work it will involve, ask yourself these questions:

1. **Is the subject big enough for a book?** *An Encyclopedia of Houseplant Care* would be. *How to water your aspidistra* wouldn't.

2. **Would the subject interest a wide enough readership to make it a commercial proposition?** Books do get written and published on some pretty obscure topics, but they're usually intended for a specialist market. It depends on how wide a readership you want to reach, and on whether it's mainly profit or prestige you want. For instance, *Advanced Theory of Semiconductors* is unlikely to outsell *A–Z of Microwave Cookery*.

3. **Is the subject one that will attract the book-buying public as well as library stockists?** The biggest potential sales are in books on self-improvement, health, food and diet, leisure activities and hobbies. Do-it-yourself titles sell well, and books on cookery and gardening waltz off the shelves. 'How-to' books are in constant demand, especially those that show how to make or save money. An American publisher, asked by a beginning writer if he thought anyone would ever write *the* 'Great American Novel', advised: 'Forget the Great American Novel. What this country needs is a good book on how to repair your own car.'

## You've got a suitable subject — so how do you tackle it?

First, break it down into manageable sections. The prospect of getting 30,000 words or more down on paper can be pretty daunting. Split it up into ten or twelve chapters of about 3,000 words each, and it loses much of its terror. It's more like writing a series of articles.

Divide your subject on paper, then, into ten or twelve sub-themes. These will eventually form your chapters. Under each sub-theme heading note all the information you already have that's relevant to that section. Make notes (in different coloured ink) of any obvious gaps in that information. You'll have to do some research to fill the gaps.

## Now comes the crunch

Do you have, or do you know how and where to find, enough material to write each of your chapters — at least 2,500 words — *without waffle or padding?* Can you realistically expect to pack every chapter with interesting and relevant information?

If not, abandon it, and look for a more suitable subject. Don't throw away your notes, though. You've probably got enough material for several articles at least.

If you're sure there's enough solid material, enough factual information for a book, then go ahead and prepare your proposal.

But don't write the book yet. If you don't find a taker for your idea, you don't want to waste your time writing an unsaleable book. If a publisher does express interest, he might want to make suggestions about the way you write the book — a different kind of treatment, perhaps, from the one you originally envisaged. If you'd already written the whole book, you would then have to do an extensive rewrite.

## HOW TO PREPARE A PROPOSAL

First, you need to make an outline of the complete book. Set down your title. The publisher might want to change it, but for the purposes of the proposal, you need a working title. Make it as snappy as you can. *How to Raise Funds for Charity* is more effective than *Organising Successful Events to Raise Money for Charitable Projects*. It would fit the spine of the book better, too.

Write down the first chapter heading, and set out underneath it, briefly, all the points you intend to deal with in that chapter.

List all your chapters in this way. Then juggle them into a logical sequence. This is the skeleton of your book, the bones on which you'll build the meat.

Type the outline neatly in single spacing, like a letter (this is a document, not a working typescript) — an extract from such an outline

Part of an outline for a proposed book: <u>How to Raise</u>
<u>Funds for Charity</u>


Introduction:
A short general overview of the choices for raising funds
as an individual, a small group, or a larger group run by
a committee.  It will also draw attention to the need to
know how the law affects various activities - this will
be covered in one of the chapters.

Chapter 1: How to set up a committee
This will show the various offices - chairperson,
secretary, treasurer and so on - and will define each
office and the responsibilities it usually carries,
stressing the importance of allocating the right job
to the right person.  For instance, it's hopeless to
appoint as Treasurer someone who can't tell an invoice
from a receipt.

Chapter 2: Fund raising and the law
What. you need to know about how much you can do without
permission, what you need permission for - for instance,
you can't sell raffle tickets door-to-door without a
special permit - and what you can't do at all.

Chapter 3: How to draw up a provisional programme of
events
Your committee needs to decide what is within its
members' capabilities and what isn't.  For instance,
there's no point in trying to organise a jumble sale if
none of your members is willing to sort out the jumble.
It's no good, either, deciding to have a brass band
concert if the nearest brass band is based a hundred
miles away and you would have to meet its travelling
expenses.                                    '

    This chapter will include a list of suggestions for
events: a summer fair, a Christmas craft fair, an
antiques and collectables fair, a car boot sale, a raffle,
an auction, a dinner dance and dozens more.

    It will also point out the areas where you need
special insurance and safety precautions.

is given on page 91. Indicate the proposed overall length of the book. If illustrations would be appropriate, say whether or not you can supply them. The publisher will advise you if he prefers to arrange this himself.

## The synopsis and sales pitch

On a separate sheet of paper, type out:

- a short, concise explanation of the book's proposed purpose and area of interest;
- your reasons for believing there's a need for it;
- an indication of the market you envisage for it;
- a few words to show that you know what the competition is like;
- your reasons for believing that your book will be better.

An example of such a synopsis is given on page 93.

Be sure to keep copies of these papers.

## APPROACHING A PUBLISHER

Look through the publishers listed in the *Writers' & Artists' Yearbook*, and draw up a list of those who specify that they handle books of the kind you plan.

Before you act on this list, ask at your library if they can access a Writers' Database on computer or if they have a copy of Whitaker's *British Books in Print*, to find out which of your proposed target publishers have recently published a book on your subject. It's best to leave those publishers off your primary target list. Unless you could offer them something radically different, your proposal would start off at a disadvantage there.

Decide which publisher you'll approach first. You should try to find out if you possibly can the name of the editor responsible for the type of non-fiction book you're going to offer. Ring up the company's switchboard and ask the operator. If the operator doesn't know, ask him or her to put you through to the editorial department for non-fiction books. Just ask for the appropriate name, and make sure you know how to spell it. Don't try to discuss your book with whoever answers the phone — all you want at this stage is the right name. *The Writer's Handbook* includes many editors' names as contacts in the various houses listed there, but it's as well to check up anyway, as publishing personnel move about a lot.

Synopsis: <u>How to Raise Funds for Charity</u>


The book will cover all aspects of fund raising, from
individual efforts (making and selling crafts, holding a
coffee morning, hosting a sales party and so on) to
large committee-run, business-sponsored events like
dinner dances and concerts.

It will be spiced with accounts of various real-
life achievements - I know of a man who raised many
thousands of pounds for a hospital by hiring Concorde
and flying a party to the USA - which will intrigue,
encourage and inspire the reader.

Legal, health and safety aspects will all be
covered.  There will be suggestions for a comprehensive
range of money-making possibilities, and a directory of
contact addresses: services, suppliers, information
sources and so on.

I believe that there are many people who would be
attracted by having so much information offered in one
handy volume.  It would be useful both to individuals
and to organisations: clubs and societies, schools and
colleges, hospital support groups, church groups and
many more.

As far as I have been able to ascertain, there are
very few publications on sale on the open market that
gather together so many facts and suggestions and combine
them with an interesting and entertaining narrative.

And one of the essential ingredients for success in
any enterprise is surely that the participants should
enjoy the venture from the outset.  The necessary
literature should also be part of the enjoyment.

## Your covering letter

This should be brief and to the point. All the information about your proposed book is in your proposal, so there's no need to repeat any of it in the letter.

If you have any special qualifications for writing the book, you should mention these — but *only* if they're relevant. Your degree in metaphysics won't persuade an editor to accept your book about fund raising — it has no relevance. Your experience in the field does, though. All you need is something on the lines of:

---

Dear Mr Corn-Harvester

I enclose a synopsis and outline of a book I am preparing about fund raising for charity. I've had fifteen years of experience in this field, both in active organisation and in administration. Would you be interested in seeing the manuscript?

Yours sincerely

---

Send the letter with the outline and synopsis, and remember to enclose an SAE.

## Prepare a sample chapter or two

You might have to wait a while for a reply, or you might have to try several publishers before you get a nibble of interest. Spend this waiting time working on a couple of sample chapters (not necessarily the first ones) and on gathering the information you're going to need to fill the gaps you noted when you were making your original notes.

When a publisher does express interest, he'll probably ask you to send him at least one chapter, so that he can see whether or not the content will live up to the promise of the proposal. He'll also want to assess your capabilities as a writer before he commits himself any further, so you must make your sample as good as you possibly can.

## When you're offered an agreement

If your sample is satisfactory, the publisher will either ask to see the completed ms 'on spec' (in which case you should think very carefully before committing yourself to finishing the book with no definite prospect of acceptance) or he will offer you an agreement on the strength of what he's already seen. With the agreement, he might also offer you an advance against royalties.

The *offer* of a book contract entitles you to apply for membership of The Society of Authors and/or The Writers' Guild of Great Britain. Either of these organisations will advise you about the agreement you've been offered, so as soon as you receive the document, contact them and they'll scrutinise it on your behalf, *before you sign it*.

You should read up on the subject of contracts, too. The Society of Authors' *Quick Guide no. 8: Publishing Contracts* is helpful, and Michael Legat's book *An Author's Guide to Publishing* has a lot of information on the topic.

## BOOKS TO HELP YOU

- Anthony Blond, *The Book Book* — gives an insider's view of the publishing world — you'll see just what's involved in selecting saleable mss.

- Raymond Hull, *How to Write 'How-To' Books and Articles* — gives practical advice and lots of detailed instruction.

- Michael Legat, *An Author's Guide to Publishing* and *Writing for Pleasure and Profit* — both good on this topic, and useful on contracts, too.

- Ian Linton, *Writing for a Living* — deals with the topic, and covers proposals.

- Dan Poynter and Mindy Bingham, *Is there a book inside you?* — how to make a book, even if you can't write it yourself. Plenty of advice and know-how.

- Gordon Wells, *Writers' Questions Answered* — deals with all the questions that trouble and confuse new writers, from 'Do I need an agent?' to 'What is a synopsis?'

## A SELECTION OF PUBLISHERS WITH STRONG NON-FICTION LISTS

- **W. H. Allen:** practical handbooks, business, reference; have always been keen on showbusiness and personality profiles, even more so now that they're associated with Virgin Books.

- **Argus Books Ltd:** modelling, woodwork, crafts, field sports, new technology, all hobbies and leisure topics.

- **B. T. Batsford Ltd:** chess, lacecraft, hobbies, animal care, fashion and costume, photography, sport, games, theatre, transport, travel.

- **Blandford Publishing:** animal care and breeding, art and graphics, humour, gardening, hobbies and crafts, sport, games, magic and the occult.

- **Century Hutchinson:** antiques and collecting, business and industry, cinema and video, DIY, sport, reference, magic.

- **David & Charles:** crafts, gardening, travel, leisure and hobbies. They'll send you their *Authors' Guide* (a handsome booklet) free on receipt of a first class stamp.

- **Mitchell Beazley Ltd:** illustrated non-fiction only — all subjects.

- **Northcote House Publishers Ltd:** business, educational, travel, self-help guides (such as this one) and general publishing.

- **Pan Books Ltd:** paperback house publishing a comprehensive range of non-fiction subjects.

- **Pelham Books Ltd:** autobiographies of sportsmen and women, sports handbooks, practical handbooks on pets, sports, hobbies, crafts and pastimes.

- **Thorsons Publishing Group Ltd:** self-improvement, health, cookery, medical, alternative medical, crafts and hobbies.

# 7
# Specialist Non-fiction

## THE RELIGIOUS PRESS

Magazines catering for all religious denominations need inspirational and educational material. Most of the religious publications in the UK are related to the Christian faith in its various denominations — *The Catholic Herald, The Tablet, Christian Herald, Church Times* and many others. *Christian Woman* and *Christian Family* serve an interdenominational readership. You'll find other religious publications listed in the *Writers' & Artists' Yearbook* and *The Writer's Handbook*, including several well-known Jewish publications like the *Jewish Chronicle* and the *Jewish Telegraph*. Many smaller religious groups publish their own papers and magazines.

If your interests lie in this direction, you're probably already familiar with the publications relating to your own faith, but you might not have thought of them as markets for your writing.

Whatever your religious persuasion, however, you should apply the same basic principles for successful writing: study each publication as an individual market, because they're all different and will look for material that satisfies their particular interests and outlook.

There's also a society for writers of specifically Christian material, The Fellowship of Christian Writers.

### Some publishers of religious and theological books

- **Darton, Longman & Todd** publish Christian books of all types, and welcome unsolicited mss, synopses and ideas for books.

- **Lion Publishing plc** publish a wide range, from board books for the very young to adult reference, all with a Christian viewpoint. They welcome unsolicited mss and ideas that are suitable for a general and international readership.

- **SCM Press Ltd** publish religion and theology, and some philosophy, sociology and current affairs. Unsolicited mss and synopses are welcome.

- **SPCK** (Society for Promoting Christian Knowledge) publish religion, theology and self-help. They prefer synopses and ideas in the first instance.

Most cities and large towns have at least one religious bookshop. You can browse in these and look for the publishers whose books reflect your own religious interests. If you can buy one or two, so much the better — you could then enlist the shop assistant or manager's help and advice about appropriate publishers.

Your library, too, should have information on religious publications.

### Books on writing for the religious press
Writer's Digest Books publish a very good book on religious writing, *Writing to Inspire* by William Gentz and Lee Roddy.

## EDUCATIONAL WRITING

You don't have to be a teacher to write educational material. Teaching experience helps, certainly, in preparing course material or textbooks, but the most important requirement is skill in communication.

The educational writer has to work within fairly strict guidelines. Content, language and structure must be geared to specific ages and abilities. You can get information on courses and required syllabus material from local authorities, career centres and libraries. If you are a teacher, you have an advantage here over the 'outsider', because you're in touch with current needs.

There are openings, however, for those with no teaching experience at all. What is needed is the ability to write well to specific guidelines.

### English language teaching
The English language is taught all over the world, not only to children but to people of all ages. Most of this teaching is done with storybooks, not textbooks. Some of these are original stories, but many are adapted from modern novels and from the life stories of famous people — Marilyn Monroe, Charlie Chaplin, Winston Churchill... Popular, too, are non-fiction subjects like airports, animals, earthquakes, the sinking of the Titanic, the Olympic Games and so on.

What's required is 'a good read' that keeps the learner turning the pages so that he absorbs the language almost without thinking about it. These abridgements and adaptations have to be prepared within tight disciplines according to varying levels of ability. At the lowest level, for example, you would work with

- a given word list of about 300 words
- a given list of simple sentence structures
- very simple tenses.

With these as your basic 'bricks', you build a story, or, for an adaptation, you use the existing storyline. You'll be asked to work within wordage limits of between 2,500 words for the lowest level to 22,000 for the highest.

---

'Adaptation is re-creation.' This is a point that was made to me when I first began writing radio drama. Later, as a producer myself, I found I had to keep making the same point to beginning writers.

A skilled adapter is a publisher's delight. Maybe you have a hidden talent for it without being aware of it. Worth a try?

Lewis Jones.

---

Lewis Jones is the series editor for Collins English Library, a series of reading books used world-wide for teaching English. He says there's a great shortage of good writers in this field, and that if you're good at it, and get a few standard works into print for world-wide circulation, you'll make your bank manager very happy.

If you think you could make a go of this kind of tightly disciplined writing, contact **Sarah Thorpe, ELT Publishing Manager, Collins Publishers**. Include your qualifications and writing experience if any, and if you have any story or adaptation ideas, mention these, too — particularly ideas for the lowest levels of ability — that's where the greatest shortage is.

The Society of Authors publishes a sixteen-page A4 duplicated set of **Guidelines for Educational Writers**, which you can buy direct from them.

### Reference books

These can be a very good publishing proposition, because they're steady sellers. There are reference books on every imaginable subject, from wildflowers to monastery sewerage systems. If you have an idea for a reference book, and enough knowledge of the subject to write it, approach a publisher with a proposal as outlined in Chapter 6.

Some other publishers of educational books:

- Cassell
- Hodder & Stoughton
- Kogan Page
- Charles Letts
- Longman
- Macmillan Educational

and of reference books:

- David & Charles
- Elm Tree Books
- Northcote House (publishers of this book).

## TECHNICAL WRITING

To be a successful technical writer, you need many of the qualities and skills of an investigative journalist. You need to know how to sift essential information from masses of data, then represent that information in terms that are easily understood by the people who need it.

To be a technical writer, you would need:

- to enjoy researching, possibly into subject matter you know little or nothing about, in enough depth to clarify the subject to people who need to understand it
- to have enough knowledge of human relationships to win cooperation from the people who hold the information you need — you might have to apply a little psychology when you deal with a temperamental genius (or even worse, with someone who thinks he's a genius)
- to possess a logical mind and a good memory
- to be able to present your findings in clear, concise, unambiguous English, without resort to specialist jargon.

It's that last point that prompts many businesses to employ writers from outside the company to prepare sales brochures, users' manuals and suchlike. Company employees can be too close to the subject to see that what is commonplace knowledge to them might be a complete mystery to the layman or non-technician. If you've ever torn your hair out over a computer handbook you'll recognise the problem. An 'outsider' sees the gaps and the areas of possible confusion because he needs to get them clear in his own mind before he can pass them on to his readers.

> In industry and commerce, who doesn't depend on their writing skills for effective interchange of information? It is the most used skill and probably the most visible gauge of individual competence. It is rarely taught (so why should we be good at it?) — how far below their potential most people normally perform is quickly realised when it is.
>
> Philip Hutton-Wilson, Head of Training, Eston Limited.

## How can you learn?

You can take a course in Technical Writing, Communication Studies or Software Documentation which will equip you with a City & Guilds qualification and the prospect of steady employment in an expanding field. A competent, qualified technical writer need never be out of work.

**The Training Division of Eston Limited** of Derby runs comprehensive MSC (Manpower Services Commission) approved courses. Eston have their own Recruitment Services, and offer active help in finding employment for their students.

## The courses

The courses are not cheap, but you might qualify for a Company Training Grant, an Armed Service Training Grant, or MSC sponsorship (Eston will apply to the MSC on your behalf, and will advise you about other grants). The 1987/88 prices for Eston Open Learning Courses were:

- Communication Techniques £299 plus VAT
- Complete Technical Authorship Course £655 plus VAT
- Software Documentation Course: at the time of writing, this course is still at the pilot stage, and prices have not yet been set.

For more information about Eston's courses and current fees, send for their Information Pack to Eston Limited, Norman House, Heritage Gate, Friargate, Derby DE1 1DD (Tel. (0332) 360202).

Much of the above information and material for the diagrams have been generously supplied by Philip Hutton-Wilson FISTC (Fellow of the Institute of Scientific and Technical Communicators), Head of Training at Eston Limited, and Chairman of the City & Guilds Scheme covering this subject.

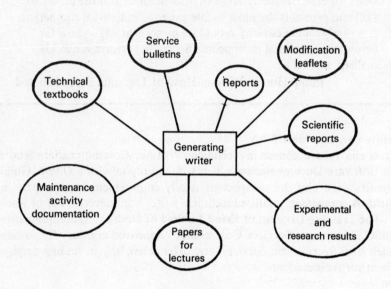

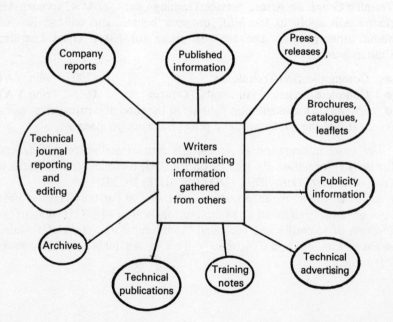

## Other courses available

**Tutortex Services** of Ulverston offer an Open Learning correspondence course in Technical Authorship. It consists of two parts, at an approximate cost (projected for 1989) of £150 per part — monthly terms are available.

Tutortex students, too, are eligible for the appropriate City & Guilds examinations, and for possible grants and sponsorship. Tutortex will advise you. They also run a self-tuition course in Technical Authorship, supplying all the teaching and self-assessment material but not the tutoring and marking given in the full course. The self-tuition course costs about £100.

For further information, details of the courses, and current costs, contact the Enrolment Secretary, A. Wilkes, Tutortex Services, 55 Lightburn Avenue, Ulverston, Cumbria LA12 0DL (Tel: (0229) 56333).

## Literature on the subject

- Bruce M. Cooper, *Writing Technical Reports.*
- J. A. Fletcher and D. F. Gowing, *The Business Guide to Effective Writing.*
- Ian Stewart, *The Business Writing Workbook.*
- Ian Linton, *Writing for a Living.*

The Society of Authors publishes a useful pamphlet, *Sell Your Writing*, which costs £1.50 direct from them. Compiled by Andrew Nash and their Technical Writers Group, this is mainly intended for business and technical writers, but gives guidelines for all writers who want fair dealing in selling their writing.

# 8
# Short Stories

You shouldn't listen too much to writers who complain that 'You can't sell short stories these days — editors don't want them...'

Comments like that are almost invariably made by unsuccessful writers who don't — or won't — recognise the true situation. The popular magazines can't get enough short stories. *Good* short stories. Well written, entertaining, *publishable* short stories.

Editorial desks groan under dull, clichéd, sermonising stories, lifeless, formless, pointless stories, sad, sordid, despairing stories... Editors don't want them. Their readers don't want them.

In 1984, when *Woman's Own* decided to stop reading unsolicited fiction, the editor, Iris Burton (she later edited *Best*), told a writers' magazine that reading the hundreds of mss they received every year was highly time-consuming and almost totally non-productive. Good short fiction was 'as hard to come by as ever', but far too few writers really study the market, she said, and to be commercially successful a writer must combine creativity with pragmatism. She had to buy much of their fiction from America, where writers take a much more professional and analytical approach.

There you have it, the key to writing successful, saleable short stories: *a professional and analytical approach.*

## TEACH YOURSELF TO WRITE STORIES THAT SELL

A saleable short story needs a structure (beginning, middle, end), a plot, a theme, sound syntax and grammar, and language appropriate to its subject and to its intended market.

You can learn how to do it. There are classes and seminars, correspondence courses, residential courses, writers' books that specialise in short-story writing. You can read, study and analyse published short stories by past and contemporary writers.

**Be ready to learn**

> Painful though it may be to a writer's ego, it is a fact of life that editors really do know what is best for their own publications, and occasionally they tell us so. Such comments may be pithy and wounding or sweet and encouraging. Whichever, take note, and never be too clever to learn.
>
> Diann Greenhow.

Diann Greenhow worked as a secretary for twenty years, then in 1984, with her children at school, and bored with 'mere housekeeping', she enrolled in a writers' correspondence course. Blessed with a diligent and compatible tutor, she has recouped the cost of the course many times over, with short stories and humorous articles sold to various publications including *Home & Country, Secrets, Red Letter* (now ceased publication), *Christian Herald, The Sunday Post*, and several 'true story' magazines. She says her acceptance rate is climbing steadily, but she still writes a lot more than she sells, and regards herself as very much a raw beginner.

If you're still dreaming of your first sale, that might seem strange, but Diann has serious ambitions to be a romantic novelist. Her successes so far, she says, are due to perseverance with her chosen markets. When her stories were rejected, she analysed them and tried to work out where she had gone wrong. Then she tried again. Gradually the rejected stories began to come back with some editorial comment instead of the usual rejection slips. She studied these comments and acted on them. And tried again. And again. Now her hard work is paying off.

## WHERE ARE THE MARKETS?

Let's look at just a few, to give you a start. Then you must dig them out for yourself, from your newsagent's shelves (make friends with him first), from writers' magazines, the *Writers' & Artists' Yearbook, The Writer's Handbook, Freelance Market News*. Don't just look at the obvious markets. Search among the specialist publications — some of these, like *British Judo, Darts World, Canal and Riverboat*, will sometimes consider short fiction that's directly relevant to their area of interest. Some regional magazines and newspapers, too, publish short stories.

## The popular women's magazines

You don't have to be a woman to write for women's and family magazines. You don't even have to write 'women's' stories. Keep up with the new publications that appear throughout the year. 1987 saw the launch of two new weekly magazines, *Best* and *Bella*, each of which features a short crime/mystery story in every issue, as well as a romance. That means slots for 208 short stories every year.

Some women's magazines prefer male writers to adopt a female pen-name, but more and more masculine bylines are appearing.

Publishers D. C. Thomson & Co. Ltd are very helpful to promising new writers. They're always on the alert for writers who can supply the right kind of fiction for their publications, which include *Annabel, My Weekly, People's Friend* and *Secrets*. They need serial stories for the weekly magazines, and short romantic or romantic-suspense novels, 35–40,000 words long, for 'My Weekly Library'. There's a regular slot, too, in the Dundee *Sporting Post*, for detective stories featuring D. C. Thomson's copyright characters 'Dixon Hawke' and his assistant 'Tommy Burke'.

---

D. C. Thomson are always in the market to find good new writers for their wide range of publications, as shown by the many different leaflets we provide.

New writers have to face the fact that competition for success is fierce. Because of the volume of contributions received, encouragement to new writers from editors can only go to those who show most promise in producing our kind of material.

Once you have studied the market, send your story to the editor of the magazine at which it is aimed or to the Central Fiction Department which acts as a clearing house for unsolicited contributions.

The Fiction Editor, D. C. Thomson & Co. Ltd.

---

Note the phrases: 'our kind of material' and 'Once you have studied the market'. You have to show not only better than adequate writing ability, but also an awareness of the company's needs. They offer encouragement and advice, not tuition in writing.

D. C. Thomson will send you their guidelines on request. These leaflets cover writing for their women's magazines, for 'My Weekly Library', and for the 'Dixon Hawke' series. They also have leaflets available on writing children's and teenage picture- and photo-story scripts, and will send you details of how to submit your mss.

## An agent

Diane Burston handles short stories, mainly for women's magazines, as well as full-length mss. She, too, remarks that it's hard to get short stories that are just right. Diane will look at a batch of up to half-a-dozen short stories, sent with a suitable SAE or IRCs, though she prefers an enquiry in the first instance. Her address is listed in the **Literary Agents** section on page 161.

## And a few more markets, for a variety of short stories

- *Acumen* magazine, editor Patricia Oxley — includes original short stories. Patricia looks for well written stories that avoid worn-out ideas and clichéd phrases.
- *Panurge* magazine, editor David Almond — almost entirely devoted to new fiction, plus a few reviews and articles about writers and writing.
- *Stand Magazine*, editors Jon Silkin and Lorna Tracy — publishes original fiction, including experimental and sometimes controversial work.
- *Interzone*, editors David Pringle and Simon Ounsley — publishes only science fiction and fantasy/horror stories.

You should *always* study at least one issue of a magazine before you send any work to it, to familiarise yourself with its style and flavour. Not every magazine, of course, will suit *your* style, and you don't want to waste either your time or theirs on unsuitable work. The magazines listed here will sell you a single copy on request.

## BOOKS ON WRITING SHORT STORIES

- Fay Goldie, *How to Write Stories and Novels that Sell* — discusses what is and what is not commercial, and gives advice on how to write saleable material. Don't be put off by the poor production (Malvern's proofreader must have been out-to-lunch that day). Fay Goldie has been writing successfully for seventy years. She's well worth reading.
- Donna Baker, *How to Write Stories for Magazines* — draws on the author's own published work and her experience to analyse the popular and more conventional magazine story.
- Paul Darcy Boles, *Story Crafting* (first published in the excellent Writer's Digest, Cincinnati, series) — discusses the art and craft of writing short stories: viewpoint, character, dialogue, style...and takes you through practical experiments to develop your writing abilities.

● Michael Baldwin, *The Way to Write Short Stories* — gives plenty
  of sound advice on plot, character, dialogue and so on. You'll
  have to dig for the nuggets, though, because the style of writing
  is idiosyncratic, even occasionally baffling.

---

**And he didn't have to wait till he was President ...**

Everybody, it seems, wants to publish a short story. Abraham
Lincoln had his published in the Quincy, Illinois, *Whig* of 15th
April 1846. 'The Trailor Murder Mystery', based on a true case,
was reprinted in the March 1952 issue of *Ellery Queen's Mystery
Magazine*.

# 9
# Your First Novel

## GETTING IT RIGHT

Publishers will heap blessings on your head if you can offer an original novel that's in tune with today's markets — better still, tomorrow's.

It can take two or three years to bring a novel from its first assessment to its appearance in the bookshops. Publishers have to be forward-thinking. So does the smart writer. You could be wasting your time trying to catch the coat-tails of yesterday's bestsellers.

The nearest you'll get to a crystal ball is to read *The Bookseller,* especially the fat Spring and Autumn numbers, each of which has about 850 pages of news and information about what is in the pipeline for the coming six months. These special issues cost about £7.50 each, but if you've made a friend of your local bookseller (and you should) he might let you browse through his copy. The weekly *Publishing News* is helpful, too.

### Be realistic

Diana Mills is a freelance interpreter/translator, journalist and copy-writer who has had short stories, poetry, reviews and plays published in several countries. Her first full-length novel, *Reapers of the Wind,* (published by Severn House in 1989), is set in Diana's native Argentina between 1950 and 1974, the era of Peron and of successive military and civilian governments. It's a story about love and the bitter struggle for survival in that turbulent country.

Diana and her agent sent the idea round several publishers, some of whom suggested changes. Eventually the idea 'came right' and was accepted by Severn House. The novel took nine months to write, and many more months of revising, tightening up, and rewriting to suit the British market. One problem was that Diana tended to take for granted a knowledge of Argentina's social customs, food and cooking, and other small details of everyday life that she had grown up with and so didn't think of describing. If the book was too 'foreign', her publishers thought, the British reader would have trouble identifying with it.

Now Diana is working on a sequel, and says that the revising and rewriting experience she gained is now proving invaluable.

---

Be realistic: the novel you want to write may not be what sells today. Markets change: study them to find out what publishers are looking for. Be open to constructive editorial criticism and above all don't lose heart. Writing a novel is like giving birth: the agony of labour vanishes with the first cry of life.

Diana Mills.

---

## A different approach

Robert Goddard approached his first novel in a completely different way. He began it in May 1983, with a rough draft of the plot. Then, over the next six months or so, he put together notes, mostly from his own experience, until he had a thirty-page summary of the projected novel. And he began to write.

He completed the first fifty pages and sent them to publishers Robert Hale, whom a friend had recommended. They were interested enough to ask to see the complete novel. It was finished in January 1985. Then came almost a year of assessment, followed by lengthy negotiations about the need to cut the overlong ms, before the contract was signed.

Robert was delighted and amazed that his first novel had been accepted by the first publisher he tried. *Past Caring* was published in 1986. It's a gripping 'I couldn't put it down' story of political and personal intrigue that reaches out from the early years of the century to ensnare characters of the present day. Its publishers regarded it so highly that they nominated it for the Booker Prize.

---

Plan your novel thoroughly from beginning to end. Then write fifty or sixty pages of it. Invest in those pages as much energy, creativity and conviction as you can summon. Type them accurately.
Package them attractively. Then try them on a publisher or agent. If there is real merit in them, it will be recognised.

Robert Goddard.

Robert Goddard's second novel, *In Pale Battalions*, a mystery story about an unsolved World War One murder, is published by Bantam Press.

## BOOKS TO HELP YOU

- John Braine, *Writing a Novel* — regarded as a classic on its subject, it's a thoroughly practical exposition of the novelist's art.
- Dianne Doubtfire, *The Craft of Novel-Writing* — practical advice and plenty of illustrative examples of how it's done.
- Fay Goldie, *How to Write Stories and Novels that Sell* — firmly focused on what is and what is not saleable.
- Paddy Kitchen, *The Way to Write Novels* — shows you the skills you need in writing prose fiction.
- Michael Legat, *Writing for Pleasure and Profit* — this excellent all-rounder is particularly good on novel-writing.
- Gary Provost, *Make Every Word Count* — a detailed analysis of how to write richly textured yet concise narrative and dialogue.
- Phyllis Whitney, *Guide to Fiction Writing* — one of the most popular writers of romantic suspense fiction tells you how it's done.

## AGENTS

The Dorian Literary Agency, the Jane Gregory Agency, and literary agent Diane Burston all handle full-length novel mss.

## 'GENRE' FICTION

You'll see references in most of the writers' manuals you'll read to 'genre' or 'category' fiction. Some 'literary' writers tend to use these terms in a slightly derogatory way, but don't let that worry you. It's no more and no less difficult to write a good 'genre' novel than it is to write a good 'general' novel. Publishers tend to divide novels into 'categories' just for ease of reference. Bear in mind, anyway, that the categories frequently overlap: 'romantic-suspense', 'spy-thriller', war-adventure' and so on. You can combine them as you wish.

How could you categorise, for instance, Douglas Adams's *Dirk Gently's Holistic Detective Agency*? *The Bookseller* defined it as 'Ghost-Horror-Detective-Whodunnit-Time-Travel-Romantic-Musical-Comedy'.

## Crime and mystery, thrillers and espionage

Most of the major publishers have crime lists, and they'll snap up a good original story — especially if you can create a character or characters who might be ripe for a series. H. R. F. Keating's 'Inspector Ghote', Ruth Rendell's 'Wexford', Reginald Hill's 'Dalziel and Pascoe', Lesley Grant-Adamson's 'Rain Morgan', Jonathan Gash's 'Lovejoy'...their sales go up with every new story.

To write modern crime stories successfully, you have to keep up to date with developments in detection methods — genetic fingerprinting, for instance. You can't afford to get left behind, or to make mistakes. Crime story mss are assessed by experts who will spot any errors or clumsy fudging. Don't risk your credibility as a crime writer by neglecting your research.

Don't be so earnest, though, that you forget that you're writing a story that people will read for relaxation and entertainment. You're not in the business of writing forensic textbooks.

---

The more I think of it the more I come to believe the key to successful fiction writing is always, on every page, with every word, to tell it to your readers. It's what all the great writers did; it's what all the bestselling writers do. Do it too.

H. R. F. Keating, President of the Detection Club.

---

H. R. F. Keating has been writing successful crime stories since the 1960s. He also writes what he calls 'mystery with history', crime novels in a Victorian setting, under the pen-name of Evelyn Hervey. In his book *Writing Crime Fiction* he shares his experience and knowledge of crime novels with new crime-writers. His advice and insights on writing will be valuable to all fiction writers, whatever their preferred genre.

In *Plotting and Writing Suspense Fiction*, Patricia Highsmith discusses her own experience of writing, charting her failures as well as her successes. She claims that the book 'is not a how-to-do-it' handbook, but in fact it's packed with detailed analyses of the techniques of mystery-suspense writing.

And no crime-writer's bookshelf is complete without Julian Symons's *Bloody Murder*, a history of crime-writing from its beginnings to the early 1980s. In the original edition, published in 1972, the author made a series of predictions about likely future trends in crime fiction. In the updated 1985 edition, he reviews what has actually happened.

## Thrills and spies

Thrillers of all kinds are big sellers. Len Deighton, Jack Higgins, Wilbur Smith, Robert Ludlum, Dick Francis all shoot straight into the best-seller lists.

Fast-moving, 'visual' writing works best. Television has conditioned thriller addicts to expect plenty of action. Long descriptive passages that used to be essential for scene-setting are boring to today's readers, who have an enormous storehouse of pictures in their memories. They don't need explanations of what a computer screen, or a race-course, or even Red Square looks like.

Spy stories have become highly sophisticated — the writing's better, too. The public's knowledge of computer-hacking for information, 'spy-in-the-sky' satellites and psychiatric drugs has made Ian Fleming's 'fairytales-with-gadgets' early Bond stories seem as unreal as 'Thunderbirds'. We've grown weary, too, of Le Carré-type 'seedy mutterings behind plywood partitions somewhere off the Charing Cross Road'. *Glasnost*, the buzzword of the decade, has given us more than just an opening up of information, it's revealed a wider imaginative field for writers who are smart enough to exploit it.

**Some publishers with good crime and thriller lists:** Collins, Constable, Gollancz, Headline, Macmillan, Robert Hale, The Bodley Head. The Women's Press publishes feminist crime and thrillers. Pandora Women Crime Writers (Pandora Press) publishes crime and mystery novels written by women (Pandora say they prefer synopses first rather than complete mss). Espionage is published by Grafton, Simon & Schuster, Hodder & Stoughton, Century Hutchinson, Collins.

**Research:** If you need specialist research for your crime novel, contact Roderick J. Richards at his agency 'Tracking Line'. A former Head of the West Midlands Police Law Research Unit, Rod specialises in biography and police and criminal history. He offers other services, including ghosting (see p.160).

**And a specialist agent:** Gregory & Radice, Authors' Agents, handle *only* crime novels and thrillers, and are particularly interested in thrillers with a political edge.

## Action-adventure, Westerns

Easy to recognise but almost impossible to define, an action-adventure story can be set anywhere in the world, in the present or in the past, even in the future, where it crosses boundaries into science fiction.

Fast-moving, full of action and excitement, with plenty of cliffhangers — these are the essentials. You need to create dynamic characters, well fleshed out and convincing enough to make the reader believe in them for the duration of the story.

**Some publishers of action-adventure:** Century Hutchinson, Grafton, Gollancz, New English Library, Viking, Collins, Bantam Press.

The Western, on the other hand, is a clearly definable genre. According to the Western Writers of America, it's a story set in the American West before the twentieth century.

If you're interested in Westerns, either writing them or reading them, you could join the J. T. Edson Appreciation Society, which will keep you in contact with other devotees and some practitioners. J. T. Edson, whose books you'll find in profusion on your library shelves, is an Englishman who has earned his living by writing Westerns for some years now. He's an authority on the history of the Old West, and a passionate champion of the Western novel.

Like popular romantic fiction, the Western is unjustly regarded with some disdain by 'literary' authors and editors. J. T. Edson says he feels he should warn aspiring writers of Westerns that editorial staff, he finds, have been conditioned from early childhood to regard the genre as substandard literature. They're disinclined to believe that an author who specialises in Westerns can possibly write anything else which will prove saleable. If you write, as J. T. does, under your own name, you might find it hard to be taken seriously should you want to break into another genre.

If you're still game to try, Robert Hale and Severn House both have Western lists.

### Science fiction

From H. G. Wells to Ray Bradbury, some of the most exciting writing in English literature explores the possibilities of life and intelligence beyond the known frontiers of time and space. Good new writers who can supply what this market needs will be welcomed with open cheque books.

If you would like to try, you could join the British Science Fiction Association which, among its many other services to its members, runs a postal workshop for beginner writers.

*Interzone* magazine, edited by Simon Ounsley and David Pringle, publishes science-fiction short stories, and keeps its readers abreast with all the best that's happening in the world of science-fiction writing.

And there's a book, *Writing Science Fiction* by Christopher Evans.

**Some science fiction publishers are:** Grafton, Headline, Gollancz (who are developing a strong list), Unwin Hyman, Methuen, and The Women's Press, who have launched the first ever women's science fiction list.

## Fantasy and horror

Don't be tempted to regard this as a 'hack' market. In an article published in 1973 in the American *Writer's Digest*, Stephen King described the genre as 'one of the most delicate known to man and it must be handled with great care and more than a little love.'

Within the accepted rules of good story-telling (that a story should be original, gripping and well-crafted) there are no restrictions. You can make magic, you can set your tale anywhere, anytime, in this world or in one of your own making. *The Lord of the Rings* is a fantasy. So is *Superman*.

But remember that a successful fantasy needs its own disciplines. It should be logical within its own terms. And above all it should tell a story. Enchanted lands, elves, monsters, mysteries and magic are only elements of a story, not a substitute for it.

If you lean towards the 'horror' side of fantasy, and enjoy reading Stephen King, Brian Lumley, Dean R. Koontz and James Herbert — in other words, if you enjoy having your blood curdled — you'll realise that the most successful horror writers play on our own fears: fear of the dark, of death, of private personal horrors like rats, bats, snakes and spiders, but most of all on our fear of the unknown.

It's an intensely personal genre. To succeed, you need total faith in what you're writing.

> Don't *always* listen to editors, and never listen to friends. A very small number of my works were improved by the suggestions of editors, but just as many have been damaged. Don't deliberately shape your work to another's design; if it's not quite right just now, come back to it when your inner man (woman) has had time to solve the problems. Remember: the road to many a moderate literary success is thick with the ghosts of friendly advice and the dust of dead friendships . . .
>
> Brian Lumley.

Join the British Fantasy Society (BFS) which covers the fantasy, horror and science fiction fields. BFS publishes a regular newsletter, a magazine called *Dark Horizons* which publishes fiction and articles, and several other magazines on subjects of interest to members. BFS also organises an annual Fantasy Conference (Fantasycon).

**Some publishers of fantasy and horror stories:** W. H. Allen, Macdonald, New English Library, Headline, Grafton, Severn House.

### Sword-and-sorcery

If you're interested in writing dungeons-and-dragons-type fantasy adventure role-playing stories, have a look at *Proteus* magazine. It's a bi-monthly with a complete game in each issue, for which they pay about £40 per 1,000 words. Editor Mike Kenward will send you guidelines on request.

### Romance, romantic-suspense, romantic-historical

Don't skip this bit just because you're a man. Romantic novelists 'Jennifer Wilde' and 'Vanessa Royall' are both men, and Mills & Boon have at least two men among their regular writers. When Mary Wibberley ran a competition for 'the best first hundred words of a romantic novel' in the hardback edition of *To Writers With Love*, the joint first-prize winners both turned out to be men writing under women's names.

There's plenty of help and advice available. You can even get an audio cassette from Mills & Boon Reader Service. They'll also send you their writers' guidelines on request — these are very detailed.

The Romantic Novelists' Association offers membership on a probationary basis, even if you've had nothing published yet. Probationary membership is conditional upon your submission of a full-length romantic novel ms as an entry in their annual Netta Muskett Award.

### Books

- Mary Wibberley, *To Writers With Love* — entertaining and challenging, a book that's guaranteed to get you writing. Mary specialises in writing for Mills & Boon, and her book is especially useful in its insights into that particular publisher's requirements.
- Jean Saunders, *The Craft of Writing Romance* — covers a wider range of romantic writing, with enlightening contributions from editors and successful writers of the genre.
- Yvonne MacManus, *You Can Write a Romance and Get it Published* — this very helpful book was published in hardback by Severn House and in paperback by Coronet. The Coronet edition has been allowed to go out of print, and there are no plans to reprint it at present. Try to get a copy of the hardback — at the time of writing Severn House still had some in stock, or it might be in your library. A dealer might be able to find a copy for you.
- Eric Partridge, *Penguin Dictionary of Historical Slang* — indispensable for writers of historical novels — it will help you avoid

those awful anachronisms of speech that crop up in otherwise well researched books.

And when you're ready, **a few publishers to try:** Collins, Century Hutchinson, Robert Hale, Heinemann, Hodder & Stoughton, Macmillan, Sphere, and of course Mills & Boon.

# 10
# Writing for Children and Teenagers

Do you have a fund of ideas for stories, informative articles, games, puzzles, jokes and picture-stories? There's plenty of room on the market for all of these — if you can write them really well.

## CHILDREN'S BOOKS

Writing for children is a very specialised business. You shouldn't make the mistake, as so many writers do, of assuming that it's easier to write for children than for adults. It isn't. You have to study the markets very closely, and work at developing the right kind of writing techniques. And those techniques will be different for each age group.

There's no room for amateurs here. Publishers receive shoals of stories with enthusiastic covering letters on the lines 'My children loved this when I read it to them — I'm sure others will, too.' Many of these mss arrive complete with unbelievably bad illustrations ('My friend has kindly done the pictures for you. She's always been good at drawing'). Unless your collaborator's work is up to professional standards, this will kill your hopes of publication stone dead.

Writing *and* illustrating a story call for professional skills far beyond the ability to entertain your own or a neighbour's children, but if you think you'd like to investigate the possibility, read Felicity Trotman's book *How to Write and Illustrate Children's Books*.

The success level in writing for children indicates that the younger the age group, the harder it is to cater for. The simpler the writing, the more skill is needed to get it just right. When you read books on the subject by successful children's writers, you'll see just how complex a discipline it is. Two of the best are *The Way to Write for Children* by Joan Aiken, and *Writing for Young Children* by Claudia Lewis.

Read these, *then* decide if you could produce the kind of material publishers want. Some teachers believe that many publishers don't really

know what children like to read. They could be right, but the writer who
wants to get his or her children's book accepted by a publisher has to
deliver what that publisher wants. (If you want to pioneer a revolution in
children's books you'll probably have to become a publisher yourself.)

Spend some time in the children's section of the library, and look at
books *recently* published by houses like the following:

- **Andersen Press Ltd** (named after Hans Christian Andersen)
  publish mostly short (32-page) books for younger children, and
  consider unsolicited mss.
- **Brimax Books Ltd** prefer to see synopses. They publish reading
  books for up to thirteen-year-olds, and board books for the very
  young.
- **Blackie Children's Books** publish picture books, fiction, fairy tales,
  folk tales and non-fiction books. They welcome unsolicited mss,
  ideas and synopses.
- **Collins Publishers** publish a very wide range of children's fiction
  and non-fiction books. They welcome unsolicited mss, ideas and
  synopses.
- **Victor Gollancz Ltd** publish fiction and non-fiction. They prefer
  ideas and synopses rather than mss.
- **Macdonald & Co Ltd** publish a wide range from board books to
  junior fiction. They welcome unsolicited mss.
- **Macmillan Children's Books** publish fiction and non-fiction. They
  welcome mss and synopses.

You'll find many more publishers of children's material listed in
the *Writers' & Artists' Yearbook* and *The Writer's Handbook*. *The
Bookseller* and *Publishing News* will keep you up to date with what's
being published.

## TEENAGE BOOKS

There's been a fast growth in this area over the last few years, with
house after house launching new imprints to cater for the teenage
market. There are great opportunities here for a writer who can tune
in to the adolescent and young teenage wavelengths. You need to be
able to write with understanding but without *any* hint of condescension,
condemnation or preaching. You need to *like* young people. If today's
teenagers horrify, disgust or alarm you, if you don't know street cred
from Street-Porter, it's probably better not to try.

Jean Saunders has a very constructive chapter on writing for teenagers
in her book *Writing Step by Step*. Jean has written successful teenage
novels herself, so she writes from experience.

## Who publishes teenage books?

You'll find the most up-to-date information in *The Bookseller* and in *Publishing News*. Look in your library, too. There's probably a special teenage section there now. Have a look at some *recent* books. You should read a few, to see what's currently marketable, before you attempt to write for this group. Check the publishers' names, and note those that publish the books that appeal to you. Note, too, the dates of first publication. You don't want to study styles, attitudes and 'in' language that have been 'out' for years.

Below are a few publishers who are currently interested in teenage and young adult books, and who will consider ideas and mss – *but* please do take note of the following caution from Richard Drew, Managing Director of Richard Drew Publishing Limited, printed with his permission:

Although we never turn away manuscripts, we prefer on the whole to deal through agents as the vast majority of manuscripts are not presented in a sufficiently professional manner and many are of mixed quality. We take on very little unsolicited material, as we have now established quite a team of good authors who can write on commission.

Richard Drew.

There again is the philosophy that's so necessary for success: you have to work at the quality of your writing, and you have to be professional in your presentation.

Richard Drew publishes the 'Swallow' mass-market paperback series of novels 'for the older child'. The four 'Swallow' titles published in Spring 1988 show the variety of the range: *Manka the Sky Gipsy* by 'B.B.' (the pen-name of writer and illustrator Denys Watkins-Pitchford) is the story of a white goose hunted in the Arctic by a determined poacher; *King Creature Come* by John Rowe Townsend is a science fiction story; *The Tournament of Fortune* by Julian Atterton is a 'quest' story set against the warfare between England and Scotland in 1314; and *The River Tree* by Mairi MacLachlan is the story of a young evacuee in the Second World War. *The River Tree* was the first unsolicited story Richard Drew accepted for the 'Swallow' series — read it, to see what qualities made it stand out from the many that have been rejected.

(Richard Drew considers only complete mss.)

The following are just a few of the other publishers who cater for the teenage market:

- **Walker Books:** teenage fiction. Approach by letter or telephone, or send ideas, synopses or complete mss.
- **Virago:** 'Upstarts', feminist fiction and non-fiction. Send the ms if you wish, but if you want to offer an idea, they need to see at least a synopsis and sample to give a good indication of what you have to offer.
- **The Women's Press:** 'Livewires'. They'll send you guidelines about their current requirements on request.
- **Penguin:** 'Puffin Plus'. Fun books, thrillers, romance, and stories about the music business. Send a synopsis and sample.

## PICTURE-SCRIPTS

Picture stories are stories told in picture form, either drawn or using photographs. The illustrations incorporate text in the form of dialogue in 'balloons', and sometimes in captions in or below the pictures.

D. C. Thomson & Co. Ltd are prolific publishers of picture-script magazines for boys and girls of all ages — *Blue Jeans, Jackie, Victor, The Beezer,* are only a few of their publications.

D. C. Thomson will send you, on request, a comprehensive pack of information about writing story scripts, and will encourage and advise you if you show promise in writing the right kind of material for them. Send for the guidelines and study them, then study some of the publications before you send in any material. Every magazine has its own distinctive characteristics, and you'll need to show an awareness of the specific requirements of any that you choose to write for. Stories are not interchangeable among the magazines.

You won't be required to supply the illustrations — these are done by commissioned artists — but you must present your script in such a way that the artist has a clear idea of what you want your readers to see in each picture.

The sample script shows you how this is done. It's the title page of a story from one of D. C. Thomson's girls' papers. You'll see that the speeches have to be very concise. There's no room in the pictures for long explanatory speeches. The text and the illustrations work together to move the story along. And don't lose sight of the fact that what you're writing is a *story*, not just a series of scenes.

## Sample script

1—Large heading picture. Leave space for title and the following introductory paragraph—

*When Gary and Lesley Stark were orphaned in a road accident, they went to live at Springbank Children's Home.*

*Gary and Lesley hoped to find a foster family where they could remain together, but had been disappointed so far. One day, Mrs Martin, the house mother, had news of a young couple who wanted to foster the twins.*

Picture shows Mrs Martin talking to the twins in her sitting room.

Mrs Martin—*Mr and Mrs Hardy seem a really nice young couple. They love children, but they haven't any of their own, so they'd like you to spend a weekend with them.*

Lesley—*That sounds terrific, Mrs Martin, but Gary and I won't build up our hopes too high. We've had a few disappointments already.*

2—**Caption**—*But at first, the Hardys did seem to be the perfect foster parents*—
Picture shows Mr & Mrs Hardy, a bright looking couple in their thirties, smiling as they lead the children from their car up the path to a small, neat terrace house with pretty front garden.

Mr Hardy—*We've been really looking forward to this weekend, kids! I hope you like our little house. It's going to be a bit of a tight fit with four people in it, but WE don't mind if YOU don't.*

Lesley—*It looks lovely, Mr Hardy, and we LIKE small houses—they're cosy!*

3—**Caption**—*Mrs Hardy showed Lesley where she was going to sleep*—
Picture shows Lesley looking puzzled as she looks around small room with nursery furniture in it. The room has clearly been meant for a baby.

Lesley—*Mrs Martin didn't tell me that you had a baby, Mrs Hardy. This room is a nursery, isn't it?*

Mrs Hardy—*Yes it is, Lesley. We did have a little baby of our own years ago, but she died, soon after she was born. We haven't had the heart to change the room since.*

4—Picture shows close-up of Lesley looking thoughtful.

Lesley—*Poor Mrs Hardy. It must have been terrible for her, to lose her baby like that. Let's hope Gary and I will be able to help her forget her sadness.*

5—**Caption**—*At tea time*—
Picture shows Mrs Hardy serving twins boiled eggs, toast strips and glasses of milk. She and her husband have meat and salad and teapot set in front of them. Lesley is sitting next to Gary, glowering at him.

Mrs Hardy—*Here we are, kiddies—nice eggies with toast soldiers, and lovely milk. If you're good, there will be stewed apple for afterwards.*

Gary—*What! B-but...oww!*

6—Picture shows Lesley smiling sweetly at her cross brother.

Gary—*You kicked me, Les. Watch where you're putting your feet.*

Lesley—*Sorry, Gary.*

(Thinks)—*I have to stop him complaining about this baby food Mrs Hardy has made for us.*

7—**Caption**—*After tea*—

Picture shows Gary and Lesley sitting in living room. The Hardys can be seen
   washing up in kitchen through the serving hatch.

Gary—*Why did they make that special baby tea for us, when they were having ham salad, Les? Do you think they were trying to save money?*

Lesley—*I expect they thought they were doing us a favour by making us a special meal. Maybe they don't realise ten-year-olds eat the same sort of food as grown ups.*

8—**Caption**—*Soon afterwards*—

Picture shows Mr Hardy standing up and looking at his watch as twins and Mrs
   Hardy look around from T.V. show they are watching. The twins look
   surprised.

Mr Hardy—*Goodness! It's half past six already! Come on, you two—time for beddy-byes!*

Gary (thinks)—*BEDDY-BYES! What's he on about? Is he bunging us off to bed at HALF-PAST SIX??*

© D. C. Thomson & Co. Ltd.
Reproduced by permission of D. C. Thomson & Co. Ltd.

## Comic strips

Almost every paper or magazine uses comic strips. If you're interested in these, either as a potential writer/artist or perhaps as a collector, contact the Association of Comics Enthusiasts, where you'll get plenty of information about comic strips past and present.

For budding authors of comic strips, there's a recently published book that should be useful, *How to Draw and Sell Comic Strips* by Alan McKenzie.

## CORRESPONDENCE COURSES

There are specialised correspondence courses in writing for children:

● **The Academy of Children's Writers** offers a tutored course, with 20 written assignments. The Academy runs no other courses. You can examine the complete printed course material, with thirty days in which to return it if you don't like what you see. The cost is about £82.50, less £10 if you pay cash up front.

● **Arthur Waite, Managing Editor of Freelance Press Services**, runs a course in Children's Authorship, covering the six-to-fourteen age group. This is a tutored course costing £85 by instalments, £75 cash.

● **The London School of Journalism** has a Writing for Children course, also tutored, at a cost of £96 by instalments, £86 cash.

All three organisations will send full details on request. The addresses are in the appendices under **Writing courses**.

# 11
# Writing Poetry, Song Lyrics and Verse

## POETRY

Poetry — the Olympic Games of writing. There's no money in it, unless you're lucky enough to win a big competition, yet the battle for publication and recognition is at its most intense here.

To take just one poetry magazine, *Outposts Poetry Quarterly* receives over 80,000 unsolicited poems every year. There's only space for fifty or so in each issue, but that doesn't stop them flooding in.

### How do you get started?

> How do you publish your poetry? Where do you start? Firstly you read other people's poetry — both contemporary and classical — sufficient to familiarise yourself with the art so that you know what you are doing. Then research the market — buy poetry books, subscribe to literary magazines. Get a clear picture in your mind of the contemporary scene, and support it, it is the one you wish to join. Finally send some of your own material off for consideration. Always typed and never without a stamped addressed envelope.
>
> Peter Finch.

Peter Finch is a poet, editor and writer of both fiction and non-fiction books, with many published volumes to his credit. He runs the Welsh Arts Council's Oriel Bookshop in Cardiff. You should read his book *How to Publish your Poetry*, a goldmine of practical advice and information that will give you a valuable working knowledge of poetry publishing. Let's look at the points he makes:

125

**Read other people's poetry:** Writing good poetry is not just a matter of setting words out in lines, like chopped-up prose. Poetry editors despair at the lack of craftmanship displayed by so many would-be poets. You need to know how to combine the various elements of poetry to achieve the effects you want. The only way to do this is to study poetry closely, to analyse how its elements work — sound, rhyming patterns, rhythm, form, all have a part to play. You can learn how to study and analyse poetry from a book like *How Poetry Works* by Philip Davies Roberts.

**Research the market:** Read what is being published today. Unless you're in touch with current poetry publishing, you can't know what editors are looking for. Too many poets are sadly out of touch. Some even insist on sending verse of the 'Prithee, I come my troth to plight' vintage to contemporary poetry magazines. It isn't that editors only want 'modern' or experimental poetry. Far from it. Good contemporary poetry takes many forms. But editors still receive hopelessly archaic verse sent by poets who seem to have read nothing written this side of the Boer War.

**Get to know the magazines you like, and support them:** Every poetry magazine has its own distinctive flavour. When you find one whose poetry is in tune with your own preferences, concentrate on that, at least to begin with. Don't even consider sending your poetry to a magazine you don't feel comfortable with, or in which you wouldn't be proud to be published. And don't send anything to a magazine you haven't seen — you don't know what kind of company you might be courting.

Subscribe to at least one magazine, more if you can afford it. It's in your own long-term interest to help keep the poetry scene alive. You need these magazines as much as they need you.

**When you're ready to try for publication:** Present your work as shown in the example on page 127, typed, single-spaced with the stanzas clearly divided, and only one poem, however short, to a page.

Put your name and address on *every* sheet — on the back if you prefer. Anne Lewis-Smith, editor of *Envoi*, says she has published several poems that arrived without identification, and keeps hoping that their authors will contact her to claim their entitlement of complimentary copies.

Never send anything (even an enquiry) without an SAE. And please don't ask for free copies 'to see if I like your magazine' or 'to study your requirements'. Small magazines struggle along on tiny budgets. Very few make even a marginal profit. You shouldn't expect them to subsidise your market study and your postage.

Unborn Children

These ghosts haunt differently, they come before,
Slowly, like secrets, pointing empty sleeves
From the margins of life, and promise more
Than the pattern anticipation weaves;
Some day I'll hear their laughter and their cries,
Touch their small hands and kiss their sleeping eyes.

They sing their coming in a swelling life,
The pleasure of our bodies' creating,
A helpless immortality my wife
And I can only tremble for, waiting
Until we hear their laughter and their cries,
Touch their small hands and kiss their sleeping eyes.

They are my laughter at the frightened years
When pain was loneliness and solitude,
My freedom from my generation's tears,
A promise of a sure familiar mood
When I hear their laughter and their cries,
Touch their small hands and kiss their sleeping eyes.

Mike Pattinson

'Unborn Children' was published in *Acumen* magazine in
October 1986, and is reproduced here in typescript form
with Mike Pattinson's permission.

## How to save money, time and aggravation

- **Don't submit work to major publishing houses.** A few, like Faber & Faber, do publish poetry, but say that they seldom find that a beginner's work meets their standards. Wait till you have a respectable number of poems in print before you think about a collection. And it's totally pointless to send single poems to big publishers.
- **Don't send poetry to magazines that never publish it.** They won't make an exception for you, however good you are.
- **Don't send a saga** the length of 'The Anglo-Saxon Chronicle' to a small magazine where it would fill a whole issue.
- **Never send the same poem to more than one magazine at a time.** This is known as 'multiple submission', and will do your reputation

no good at all. You risk a double acceptance — not the triumph you might think. The editors concerned will be mutually embarrassed, and won't forgive you easily. Don't imagine they won't find out. Poetry editors see a lot of poetry magazines, and even if they didn't see the gaffe for themselves, you can be sure some indignant poet will 'advise' them.

## POETRY 'ON THE AIR'

Poet Peggy Poole produces and presents BBC Radio Merseyside's regular poetry programme 'First Heard'. Peggy has written the following guidelines for you, from her experience of selecting poems suitable for reading 'on the air':

### Outlets
If your local BBC or independent radio stations have no poetry programme, ask for one and organise area support. Station managers need persuading that poetry is an active part of life today; many still regard it as 'soft' or childish and think in terms of doggerel.

### Submission
Submit as for a top-class magazine, with an SAE. Keep poems relatively short — a rough line limit of forty. (This does not mean the total exclusion of any longer work, particularly of a possible dramatic poem for several voices. In such a case it would be wise to write to the producer in advance explaining the content, and a decision will be made either to present an extra, one-off programme or to vary the style of the regular poetry programme for that one special occasion.)

Do not use four-letter words even if they are an integral part of a poem; this will jeopardise the programme.

Keep off politics, and ensure seasonal work arrives with plenty of time in hand. Humour is welcomed provided it is genuinely poetic and does not belong to a comedy programme. It's best to avoid nostalgic or pseudo-religious poems — huge amounts of these are received, but hardly ever used.

### Reading
Many poets want to read their own work, but studios at the average broadcasting station are usually too heavily booked for this to be possible; but it will depend on the producer and the format and length of the programme.

### Payment
Do not expect this to be more than a token payment.

A good poem should work as well on radio as in print, but it is important to remember that your audience is probably engaged in several other occupations while listening, so your poem needs to work instantly at one level while offering resonances of deeper meaning at the same time. In producing BBC Radio Merseyside's poetry programme I balance on a tight-rope, aiming both to attract the established poet without intimidating new poets from submitting their first attempts, and to present an enjoyable half-hour that might also succeed in converting a newcomer to poetry.

Peggy Poole.

### Study this market, too

Listen to as much broadcast poetry as you can. At the time of writing, the BBC is in the throes of a 'shake-up' of sound broadcasting, so we don't know what their future policy on poetry will be. There should be some information in the new edition of *Writing for the BBC*, promised for 1988, and details of poetry programmes are given in *Radio Times*.

(Please note that the information service offered by the Association of Independent Radio Contractors, which is referred to in the *Writers' & Artists' Yearbook* up to the 1988 edition, has been discontinued.)

You might like to see the kind of poetry that's considered suitable for broadcasting on local radio. Peggy Poole has edited a booklet of poems from her programme, 'First Heard'. See under **Useful booklets**.

---

### CHECKLIST FOR POETRY SUBMISSIONS

1. Each poem is typed in the accepted form on a separate sheet of plain white A4 paper.

2. Your name and address appear on every sheet.

3. You've kept a note of where you're sending each poem, so that you don't risk a multiple submission.

4. You've enclosed a stamped addressed envelope big enough and bearing enough postage for the return of the whole batch.

---

## SOURCES OF INFORMATION AND ADVICE

● **The Association of Little Presses** (ALP) issues *Poetry and Little*

*Press Information* (PALPI), and a current catalogue of *Little Press Books in Print*.

- **The Friends of the Arvon Foundation** produce a regular newsletter of information about competitions, festivals, writers' markets and literature.
- **The National Poetry Foundation** offers to members news of competitions and publications, and runs a poetry appraisal service for members.
- **The Oriel Bookshop** publishes *Small Press and Little Magazines of the UK and Ireland* (a regularly updated address list), a catalogue of recent poetry publications, a regular programme of literary events, a mail order 'books on books' service, and *for writers living in Wales only*, a criticism service subsidised by the Welsh Arts Council.
- **The Poetry Society** issues *Poetry Review Quarterly*, and also an information bulletin, advance notification of all Poetry Society events, access to special offers from the Poetry Society Bookshop, and a critical service which anyone can use, although society members get reduced rates.
- **The Poetry Book Society** (a book club) offers a *Quarterly Bulletin*, a free annual *Poetry Anthology*, and discount prices on quality poetry books.

## Books

- Peter Finch, *How to Publish your Poetry* — probably the best investment you could make, full of information and practical advice.
- Michael Baldwin, *The Way to Write Poetry* — includes practical basic advice for beginners.
- Philip Davies Roberts, *How Poetry Works* — shows how to understand the ways in which the various elements of English poetry — language, rhythm and metre, rhyming patterns and so on — contribute to a poetic work.

## Magazines

Here are a few titles to introduce you to the wide range available. As you become more familiar with the poetry scene you'll discover many more.

- *Acumen*. Two issues a year. Well produced and printed. Publishes poetry, prose, reviews, interviews, articles on poets and poetry. 100-plus pages. Editor Patricia Oxley has no preferences on form or content, but you should avoid clichéd subjects.

- *Envoi*. Published three times a year. New poetry, news and reviews.

Editor Anne Lewis-Smith prefers fairly short poems (up to about forty lines). There's a competition in every issue. Rejected poems are returned with a line or two of constructive criticism. No experimental poetry, and no strong language. Well produced, professionally printed. 40 pages.

- *First Time.* Published twice a year. Neatly printed production, devoted to new poetry by new poets. Editor Josephine Austin.

- *Outposts Poetry Quarterly.* Professionally produced and printed. Publishes a broad range of poetry by both new and established poets, and news and reviews. Now edited by Roland John, following more than forty years under the stewardship of the late Howard Sergeant MBE. 70-plus pages.

- *Prospice.* An international literary quarterly, 160 pages long, publishing original poetry, short prose and reviews. *Prospice* has a policy of publishing several poems at a time by each contributing poet, not single poems, so you should send batches of half-a-dozen or so. Poems sent in by unknown poets are considered in exactly the same way as those sent by established poets — they're chosen on merit alone. The editors are J. C. R. (Jim) Green and Roger Elkin.

- *Stand.* An international quarterly of new writing, publishing new poetry, fiction, plays, translations, criticism and art, and reviews of new poetry and fiction. Left of centre, and 'hospitable to a wide range of work. Free from prejudice, but socially conscious' the editors promise. They look for well-made but exploratory writing. There's a lively readers' letters feature, and lots of advertisements and information about literary publications. 80 pages. Editors Jon Silkin and Lorna Tracy.

- *Writers' Own Magazine.* Duplicated production. Poetry and prose, almost all by new or relatively new writers. Some news and reviews. A readers' letters section mostly providing mutual encouragement for its contributors. A useful starting point for beginners. Editor Eileen M. Pickering.

- *The Writers' Rostrum.* Also a duplicated production. Poetry and prose, mostly by new writers. News and reviews, and occasional articles about writers and writing. Very friendly. Editor Jenny Chaplin.

- *Writing.* Another privately produced duplicated writers' magazine. Friendly, with news and reviews of competitions, books and so on. Articles by writers about writing, and a few poems, short stories and articles by new writers. Editor Barbara Horsfall.

# SONGWRITING

Do you dream of writing a 'standard', another 'White Christmas' or 'Stardust'? Did you watch the 'Song for Europe' contest and think 'I could write something better myself'? And maybe you could. From folk to funk, from traditional to pop, there's always room for a good new song.

*'Somebody called Lloyd Webber wants to talk to you.'*

## You can't write music?
You don't have to. What you need is a collaborator. You write the lyrics, your collaborator writes the music, and you take equal shares of any profits.

## Look out for sharks
The 'shark' is the music business's equivalent of the vanity publisher. He asks for payment to write music to your lyrics. Don't fall for this. There hasn't yet been a successful song produced in that way. You'd be throwing your money away.

## So how do you get started?
You can join a professional organisation, even if you're an absolute unpublished beginner. You'll have access to sound *professional* advice and guidance. If you need a collaborator, you'll be helped to find one who will work with you, on equal terms, with no money changing hands in either direction unless and until your song makes a profit.

The **British Academy of Songwriters, Composers and Authors** (BASCA) offers Associate Membership to unpublished songwriters. (Please note that the 'Authors' in the name refers to lyric-writers.) Associate Membership costs £11.50 per year. For this, you have access to BASCA's advice and guidance services, and you'll receive a quarterly information bulletin, *BASCA News*. For full details of BASCA membership and services, contact the General Secretary, Marilyn Worsley, at the address given in **Associations and Societies Open to Unpublished Writers** on p. 152.

**The Society of International Songwriters & Composers** (SISC) offers full membership to both amateur and professional songwriters. SISC services to members include song assessments, collaboration between lyric-writers and composers (SISC keeps a register of collaborators), information on music publishers' requirements, advice on copyright, contracts and so on. Members receive a free quarterly magazine, *Songwriting and Composing*. Membership costs £12.00 per year. Contact the Chairman, Roderick G. Jones, at the address given in **Associations and Societies Open to Unpublished Writers** on page 152. SISC has an associated music publishing company, First Time Music (Publishing) UK Ltd, at the same address.

### And there are books

- Stephen Citron, *Songwriting* — takes you step by step through writing a song, illustrated with words and music from well-known songs. Full of ideas and 'tricks of the trade', it's particularly helpful for beginners. Covers lyrics, music, rhythm, rhyme, form and style.
- Sheila Davis, *The Craft of Lyric Writing* — a guide to the art of writing words for and to music. Works through examples, and shows how to avoid common pitfalls.

## GREETING CARD VERSES

This is where you scout around your newsagent's again, but now you're interested in his display of greeting cards. Greeting cards are very big business. According to recent figures from America, their citizens send out over 10,000,000 'conventional' greeting cards *every day of the year*. And 'conventional' cards are only one category of the six basic types of card. The others are 'informal', 'juvenile', 'humorous', 'studio' and 'inspirational'.

There's an expanding market here in the UK, too, for greeting cards, and quite a few of the card companies buy ideas and verses from freelance writers.

Study the cards that take your fancy — could *you* think up ideas like that? Could you write the kind of verses the 'conventional' and 'inspirational' cards print? Look at the back of the cards. You'll often find a company name there, and sometimes the full address and telephone number. This is where you take the initiative. Ring them up, or write to them, and ask if they consider freelance material and ideas. Then if you get the 'go-ahead', send them some of your own work.

You can present an idea for, say, a humorous or novelty card in simple terms in a letter. A verse or slogan, however, should be sent on a 3″ x 5″ or 5″ x 7″ piece of strong paper or light card, laid out as it would appear on the printed card. Then on the back of the paper or card type your name and address, and an identification code for that verse or idea:

Front:                                      Back:

I wish you a garden                         CV/23
Where bluebirds fly free,
A carpet of clover,                         Marigold Bloom
A copper-leaf tree.                         7 Lush Lane
                                            Marshfield
Our hearts will make music
As sweet as the flowers,
When we walk together
In love's golden hours.

Send your verses or ideas in batches of six or eight, and remember to enclose an SAE.

If a greeting card company likes the kind of work you send them, even if they don't accept anything right away, they'll probably add your name to their list of contributors, and send you regular information about their current requirements. You can earn a useful amount of money. Most companies pay upwards of £20 for a single verse. American markets often pay more.

You can find information about American greeting card companies in the annual American *Writer's Market*, which you can get from Freelance Press Services.

You can get information about UK companies from the Greeting Card and Calendar Association — *see* **Information services and sources** on page 159.

# 12
# Writing for Radio, Screen and Stage

## RADIO AND TELEVISION

The British Broadcasting Corporation (BBC) is one of the biggest potential markets for freelance writers. There's a lot of competition, however, and the BBC receives far more scripts in all its departments than it can possibly accept. Everything sent in is read, though, *except* that BBC Television 'can offer no market for unpublished novels, short stories, biographies, autobiographies, etc., and consequently is not willing to read and consider them'. So states *BBC Television Market Information for Writers*, a set of notes that you can get on request from the Television Script Unit. So don't waste your time sending your short stories in the hope that a scriptwriter will adapt them into screenplays. They won't be read at all. Send for these notes — they give detailed guidance on the different kinds of material currently wanted for all the various BBC TV outlets: plays, serials, light entertainment, children's programmes, school broadcasting and so on. There's a sample script layout, and a list of recommended books.

Radio Four's 'Morning Story' slot uses good short stories of between 2,300 and 2,500 words, and many of these are written by freelances.

There's a big demand for radio plays for the various drama slots, like 'Afternoon Theatre', 'Saturday Night Theatre' and the many half-hour play broadcasts. The Script Editor (Radio Drama), BBC, Broadcasting House, London W1A 1AA will send you a free leaflet, *Notes on Radio Drama*.

There are some openings for talks and features, but there's usually a fair backlog of material in hand for those.

The *Writers' & Artists' Yearbook* gives information about broadcasting rights and terms, and lists addresses of BBC and Independent radio and TV stations. *The Writer's Handbook* gives a great deal of detailed information about the personnel of BBC and Independent radio and TV stations, film and video companies, and their various requirements — this would be a good investment if you're seriously interested in writing for these media.

---

If you have no track record don't start by writing for TV drama, *except for fun* — you'd have more chance of winning the pools than having your play bought and transmitted.

The best market for new playwrights is without a doubt BBC Radio. The best slot length is half hour, followed by Afternoon Theatre (45 or 55 minutes).

If you are an intellectual giant write half hour plays for Radio 3, they are always desperate for a good product.

If you have a sense of humour let it show in your scripts. 'Funny' is more saleable than 'Doom and Gloom'.

Don't waste time entering competitions — back to winning the pools again — simply send your first script, typed, double spacing, A4 paper, good sized left margin, off to BBC Script Unit, BBC Broadcasting House, London W1A 1AA, then get on with writing the next. No point in waiting to see how they like the first — it's going to be three months before you hear about that one, unless it's an absolute 'No-no' when it will be back in two.

The only book on the subject I would advise buying is *Writing for the BBC,* a BBC publication that gives all available markets, plus demonstration layouts.

See — easy, isn't it?

Wally K. Daly, Chair, Writers' Guild of Great Britain (writer of drama and situation comedy for both radio and TV; also of five stage plays and three musicals, the best known being *Follow the Star* (music, Jim Parker)).

---

## Is the money good?

Yes, it can be very good, especially if you can establish yourself as a valued regular contributor. What you'll be paid depends on how well established you are. For example, the BBC's short-story payment starts at £82 for a fifteen-minute story by a beginner. A writer who has six or more short stories to his credit is paid £107. A beginner in radio drama should get £915 for a sixty-minute script, but a regular writer would get £1,386 minimum.

● The minimum rates negotiated by the Writers' Guild for a sixty-minute television play are £2,673 to a beginner, £4,212 to a regular writer. (ITV rates are almost one third higher.)

## Comedy and light entertainment

The most exciting recent development in comedy and light entertainment writing has been the establishment, in the early 1980s, of the Comedy Writers Association (CWA). The CWA was formed to promote good comedy writing and to encourage and advise new writers. CWA members sell to radio and TV outlets worldwide. They're helped by the lively exchange of experiences, techniques and market information.

Writing saleable comedy material is a very specialised discipline. You have to know what's wanted where and at the right time.

---

Every comedian has his own style. Study that style and tailor your work to suit. For example, a joke written for Ken Dodd would be no good for Roy Walker. In situation comedy, keep characters and sets to a minimum. Avoid too much outside filming. Study TV programmes and comedians. And accept rejections — they're part of every comedy writer's life.

Ken Rock, President, Comedy Writers Association.

---

As well as Ken Rock, writers Wally K. Daly, Alan Bond, Joyce Lister, Steve Wetton, John Brown and Richard Halford — who have contributed material to this book — are all members of the CWA.

## Don't leave it all to the men

Why is it that most women assume that only men can write funny material? You'll probably find it quite hard to think of more than a handful of women who have made their mark in comedy writing. Victoria Wood, of course, Carla Lane, French and Saunders...But not many more.

---

For centuries women have laughed at jokes told and written by men. Yet despite being successful as writers, few women attempt to write comedy. Being a keen observer of human nature, seeing the funny side of life and the ability to study comedy writing techniques is not exclusive to men.

Joyce Lister.

---

Joyce Lister is building a successful second career as a comedy

writer, after illness forced her to give up her nursing activities. She
has sold material to (among other outlets) *The Grumbleweeds* (Granada
TV), *Fast Forward* (BBC2 for children), Little and Large, and Radio
Luxembourg. She's also a talented and successful writer of greeting card
material. Joyce is one of the growing number of women members of the
Comedy Writers Association, and would like to see more women writing
in this field.

Have you got Joyce's kind of talent? If you think you have, and you'd
like to try, contact the CWA and find out more about it.

## A specialist service

Rosemary Horstmann brings her long experience and expertise as a
producer, broadcaster, scriptwriter, journalist, tutor and administrator
to a service designed to give constructive advice and supportive
encouragement to authors who want to write for broadcasting.

Rosemary offers script evaluation, coaching in interviewing techniques, and tuition in the use of a professional tape recorder and the
editing of tape. Tuition sessions on script-writing and her other services
can be arranged either one-to-one or on a group basis. The charges
are:

● script evaluation, from £20 per script, depending on length and
  complexity
● consultancy/individual tuition, £20 per hour
● groups and workshops by arrangement.

Rosemary will send you full details of her service on request.

## Recommended reading
● *Writing for the BBC*, published by the BBC itself.
● William Ash, *The Way to Write Radio Drama*. Written by a very
  experienced BBC script editor, and covers the whole field of radio
  drama.
● Brad Ashton, *How to Write Comedy*. A practical and entertaining
  guide to writing comedy, from one-liners to situation comedy.
  (Required reading for intending CWA members.)
● Rosemary Horstmann, *Writing for Radio*. Practical advice from a
  very experienced producer, writer, tutor and lecturer.
● William Miller, *Screenwriting for Narrative Film and Television*.
  Narrative structures, settings and dialogue, with examples from well
  known screenplays.
● Eric Paice, *The Way to Write for Television*. A guide to the
  necessary disciplines, approaches and presentation, and how to
  avoid the pitfalls. The new edition is revised and updated.

- *The Stage and Television Today.* The entertainment world's newspaper.

## WRITING FOR FILM AND VIDEO

Most film and video companies will only look at material submitted through an established agent. You could try contacting one of the agents listed in the *Writers' & Artists' Yearbook* and *The Writer's Handbook*. Make sure you choose only those who specify an interest in this field. Your chances are slim, however, unless you can present some reasonably impressive work-in-progress and preferably also a portfolio of published work. They're not really likely to be interested in a total beginner.

As a newcomer, your best first move is to send for details of the London Screenwriters Workshop. Although this association is based in London, it caters for many out-of-town and overseas members, too. And you don't need any track record to join.

## WRITING FOR THE STAGE

Your best starting point as a new playwright is a local repertory theatre or amateur dramatic group. If you have no track record at all, it's unrealistic to expect to see your name in lights in London's West End with your first effort. Not impossible, but not likely.

*Well, you can dream, can't you?*

However, management companies send scouts to repertory productions all over the country. They're always on the lookout for original and potentially profitable plays, and yours might be 'spotted'.

It's usually best to write first and ask if the company would like to see your script. Give all the relevant details: type of play, how many sets, how many characters and so on.

*Never send anyone your only copy.*

Read up on production contracts *before* you sign any agreement. The *Writers' & Artists' Yearbook* explains agreements in detail.

### Playwrights' groups

Ask your nearest Regional Arts Council office (phone numbers and addresses are in the *Writers' & Artists' Yearbook*) for details of any **playwrights' association** in your area. Most of these groups hold readings and can arrange for script criticism.

The **Players & Playwrights Society** holds meetings on most Monday evenings at St John's Church Hall, Hyde Park Crescent, London W2. The society is made up of amateur and professional writers and actors, and its function is to let writers hear their plays read, and to give actors the chance to act out new plays as readings.

Membership of the **New Playwrights Trust (NPT)** is open to all playwrights and aspiring playwrights, and all those interested in developing and encouraging new playwriting. They issue a monthly newsletter, and members can use the NPT information services (contracts, theatre companies' policies, competitions, grants, venues and more). There's a script library, and for a modest fee there's a script criticism service.

### Getting your play published

It's well worth trying to get your play published, especially if it's been considered good enough to be given live performance by a local company. You can send your script to **Samuel French Ltd**, who publish nothing else but plays. If French's publish it, they'll include it in their *Guide to Selecting Plays*, a substantial catalogue of plays intended for performance by amateur dramatic groups.

You don't need an agent to approach French's, but they do prefer that the play should have been tried out in some kind of performance, because that reveals flaws that might have been overlooked in the written work, and which you could then correct before submitting the piece for professional consideration by their readers. They make no charge for assessing scripts.

The *Guide to Selecting Plays* costs £2.95 post paid. French's will also send you, on request and free of charge, their mail order lists of books and cassettes on all the media and performing arts: writing, acting, production, make-up and so on, from Shakespeare to pantomime. (It helps if you can specify your area or areas of interest.)

## Theatre production companies

You could try making direct contact with some of the dozen or so professional production companies who actively seek new writers' work. There's a useful section on theatre companies in *The Writer's Handbook,* which gives more details than the *Writers' & Artists' Yearbook* on this topic. Stick to companies who specify an interest in new writing.

## Specific requirements

Production companies, like book and magazine publishers, have their own individual styles and requirements. Very few plays would suit them all. Make a point of finding out as much as you can about a company's preferences before you approach them. This groundwork could pay good dividends. Study the entries in *The Writer's Handbook,* and read *The Stage and Television Today*, the weekly newspaper of the performing arts. These will give you a good idea of what production companies are interested in. Keep an eye on the small ads in *The Stage and Television Today,* where you'll sometimes find small companies asking for scripts.

When you're sending a script to a production company, you should use the standard layout. Make it quite clear who is saying what, and which lines are speech and which are stage directions. Study the sample script on page 142, an extract from Steve Wetton's play *King of the Blues.*

Steve also offers you this tip: Nowadays, directors and actors tend to fall about laughing when they see the kind of detailed stage directions that used to litter playscripts. Directions like 'Jeremy moves downstage right, knocks his pipe out in the ashtray to the left of the paperweight and then goes to lean nonchalantly with his right elbow on the shelf above the mantelpiece' are a total giveaway of a writer's inexperience.

There's a helpful booklet you can send for, *The Playscript from Scratch*, compiled by David Huxley. It's a beginner's guide to preparing and marketing a script, with explanations and examples of the accepted playscript format, and information about copyright, study courses, grants, literature and more.

## Grants and bursaries

The Arts Council of Great Britain gives details of various forms of financial assistance in their brochure *Theatre Writing Schemes.* For

## ACT ONE SCENE 4

*(Into Daniel's fantasy) The stage remains in total darkness for a few seconds. Then we hear a voice off. It is Daniel's own voice but distorted and amplified to sound God-like.*

VOICE: In the beginning there was the stadium. But the stadium was empty and the ground without shape or form.

*There is a roll of thunder and a flash of lightning lights up the stage for a second. We see a deserted football stadium.*

Darkness was everywhere. Then the spirit of God moved in the wilderness and said: Let there be light.

*Lights up. But they are floodlights as at a football stadium.*

This was the first day and it was good. But God saw that the stadium was empty and the gates were poor so he didst command: Upon these terraces let there come forth all creatures great and small.

*Football fans enter. Bewildered at first. Newly born.*

And he called these creatures *(pause)* fans.

*Explosion of noise. Cheering etc. It stops as suddenly as it began.*

Then God blessed these creatures and said unto them: Go forth and multiply.

FAN: He said what?

VOICE: You heard. Go forth and multiply.

FAN: Right, lads. Let's get at it. *(They try)*

VOICE: And this was the second day and it was good. *(Pause)* But not that good for he had not yet invented women. *(Groans from fans).*

FANS: *(Chant)* Why are we waiting? Why are we waiting...?

Reproduced with permission from Steve Wetton's play *King of the Blues*, performed at the Derby Playhouse. Not yet published.

a copy of the brochure and further information, contact the Drama Director, The Arts Council of Great Britain. Or you could enquire at your local Arts Council Office.

Here are the detailed requirements of three companies who welcome new plays:

### Paines Plough, The Writers' Company

Produces nothing but new writing. A Readers' Panel reports on all scripts submitted (this can take two or three months). They offer you the following tips about submitting mss:

- DO take care with the layout. It's especially important to distinguish between dialogue and stage directions. Underline all stage directions *or* type them in capitals.
- DO put the full name of the character (not an initial or other abbreviation) in capitals on the left hand side of the page before every speech. Spread out generously. *Never* use both sides of the paper.
- DO enclose a suitably sized SAE.
- DO include a brief synopsis, fewer than 200 words.
- DO make the cover of the play look interesting in some way.
- DON'T send more than one play at a time. The envelopes that collect most dust are the ones containing 'a selection' of the author's work. Find out about the company you're writing to and send them the play you think most appropriate — if they want more, they'll ask for more.
- DON'T say too much in your covering letter. Avoid a detailed explanation of your play's themes and meaning — if these are not clear in the play itself, then you've written it badly.
- DON'T waste a fortune in postage. Send out a synopsis with a sample scene, and find out which companies are really interested.
- DON'T pester people. Wait at least three months before enquiring about a response.

### The Traverse Theatre, Edinburgh

One of the country's foremost producers of unknown work by new writers. They read everything that comes in, but they say it helps if authors keep to a few basic requirements:

- DO limit the cast to not more than nine characters. Include a character list and the number of actors required.
- DO include a line or two on the setting ('London in the Blitz', 'contemporary living room' and so on).

- DO remember that small underfunded theatres like the Traverse can't do spectacular effects with swimming pools, live animals and the like.
- DO note that the company looks for plays that say something new. There would be little interest in scripts about mid-life crises set in kitchen and living room, for instance.
- DO please use some kind of binding. Readers take piles of scripts home to read — and loose scripts don't mix with children and pets.

Any play you submit to the Traverse Theatre should not have been performed professionally before. Send the full script, not a synopsis.

You'll receive a reader's report from a panel of directors, actors, writers and academics. This can take up to three months, so be patient. Perhaps one author in twenty will be asked to see them. One in 500 might get a workshop reading, and one in 1,000 a full production. If your play is thought to be good but not suitable for the Traverse, they'll advise you about other possible outlets.

### The Liverpool Playhouse

Has an active policy of promoting new work in both its auditoria, the Mainhouse which seats 750 (it's an old music hall theatre), and the Studio, which seats 100 and works to any configuration.

The Playhouse is looking for exciting, innovative work from new playwrights, 'the voice of the 80s and 90s', with a real feeling of truth in the writing. The company is particularly supportive to local writers through workshops and writer surgeries. These are a few guidelines:

- All new scripts are welcome. They are read by a pool of readers who then submit reports to the Associate Director, Kate Rowland.
- Scripts can be sent straight to the theatre — no letter or synopsis is required. Everything should be very clearly addressed.
- Scripts should be typed, with all pages numbered.
- There are no stipulated criteria in terms of content, cast size and so on, but huge casts are difficult.

### Recommended Reading

French's Theatre Bookshop will send you a list of books relevant to writing for the theatre. A recent book in the Elm Tree series is Tom Gallacher's *The Way to Write for the Stage*, which covers advice about the choice of subject, the action of the play, its structure, using the stage, dialogue, rehearsal, contracts, agents, adaptations and so on.

# Glossary

**Advance** A sum paid to an author in advance of publication of his book. The usual terms are that the publisher will retain the author's royalty until the advance is paid off, after which the author receives his agreed share of profits.

**Agreement** See **Contract**.

**Anthology** A collection of stories, poems and so on, which may or may not have been published before.

**Article** A piece of prose writing that deals with a single subject (less commonly with several related subjects).

**Autobiography** A person's life story, written by himself.

**Balloon** A balloon or bubble-shaped outline containing text.

**Bi-monthly** Every two months.

**Biography** An account of a person's life as investigated and evaluated by someone else.

**Blurb** Promotional text on the flap of a book jacket or the outside back cover of a paperback, sometimes exaggerating its worth.

**Bullet** A large dot used to precede and add emphasis to an item in a book or article. Also called a stab point.

**Byline** A line at the head or foot of a piece of writing identifying the writer: 'by Adam Ampersand'.

© A symbol signifying that a work is protected by copyright.

**'Category' fiction** Fiction written to fit into a specific genre: romance, Western, thriller and so on.

**Collaboration** The working together of two or more people to produce a work, sometimes published under a single pseudonym. (For example, 'Ellery Queen' who is/are Frederic Dannay and Manfred B. Lee.)

**Contract** A signed document, an agreement between publisher and author specifying in exact detail the responsibilities each party undertakes in the writing, production and marketing of a book, in terms of payment, assignation of rights and so on.

**Copy** Matter to be typeset. Usually refers to the prepared typescript.

**Copyright** The exclusive right in his own work of an author or other designated party, as defined by law.

**Copywriting** Writing material for use in advertisements, publicity material and the like.

**Critique** A critical examination and written report on a work.

**Deadline** The latest date or time by which a job must be finished.

**Draft** A preliminary version.

**Edition** One printing of a book. A second or subsequent edition will have alterations, sometimes substantial, compared to the previous edition.

**Editorial policy** The editor's overall concept of the kind of publication he wants to produce.

**FBSR** First British Serial Rights. The right to publish a story or article for the first time and once only in the UK. Not applicable to books.

**Feature** A magazine or newspaper piece, an article which is not one of a series.

**Fiction** Writing that is not and does not pretend to be truth, but which is entirely drawn from the imagination.

**Flyer** A leaflet sent out in the post.

**Folio** 1. A leaf, that is, two pages of a book. 2. A page number. 3. A manuscript page.

**'Freebie'** A slang term for a freesheet, a publication distributed free to householders, travellers and so on. Anything given without charge.

**Freelance** A self-employed person who sells his or her services or written work to a publisher for an agreed fee. A writer/journalist who sells work to various publications but is not employed by any one publisher. (Derives from the mercenary knights and soldiers who wandered Europe after the Crusades, hiring out their services, complete with lances, wherever they could.)

**Genre** A literary species or specific category, for example Westerns, detective stories and so on.

**Ghosting/ghost-writing** Writing a book in conjunction with someone else (usually a celebrity but could be anyone with a saleable story) as if it had been written by that other person, with no credit given to the writer.

**GSM** Grammes per square metre (grammage), the specification of paper weights.

**Hack** A slightly derogatory term applied to a person who writes primarily for money.

**HB** Abbreviation for 'hardback', a book with a stiff board cover.

**Imprint** 1. The name of the printer with the place and time of printing, required by law in many countries for papers, books and so on meant for publication. 2. The name of the publisher with place and date of publication.

**IRC** International Reply Coupon, a voucher sold at post offices worldwide, equivalent to the value of the minimum postal rate for a letter posted in the country from which the reply will come.

**ISBN** International Standard Book Number, a unique ten-digit reference number given to every book published, to identify its area of origin, publisher, title and check control.

**ISSN** International Standard Series Number, an eight-digit reference number given to periodical publications, used in a scheme analogous to the ISBN system.

**Journalist** A person who writes for a journal, newspaper, periodical and so on, as distinct from authoring books.

**Layout** The overall appearance of a script, or a printed page.

**Libel** A printed or broadcast malicious and defamatory statement.

**Literary agent** A person who acts on behalf of an author in his dealings with publishers, offering his work and negotiating the contracts for work he places. Agents always work on commission, usually 10–15%. They don't make any money from your work till you do.

**Mainstream fiction** A term applied to literary subjects that are traditional or current, as distinct from category or genre fiction.

**Market study** The analytical study of the author's possible points of sale.

**Matter** Either manuscript or other copy which is to be printed, or type that is composed for printing.

**Media** Sources of information, such as newspapers, magazines, radio, TV and so on. (Plural of medium, that is, 'medium of communication'.)

**Multiple submissions** The sending of the same ms to more than one publisher at a time. In general, this is not an acceptable practice.

**Novel** A fictional story written in prose, of any length but not usually less than 50,000 words.

**'On spec'/on speculation** Usually applied to writing submitted to an editor on a purely speculative basis, that is, not by invitation or commission. Also applied to work sent at an editor's invitation but without any commitment from him to accept the piece.

**Outline** A sketched-out structure of a piece, showing all it will contain and in what order, but without going into detail. See also *synopsis*.

**Out of print** No longer on the publisher's list, that is, no longer available except from libraries or second-hand book dealers.

**'Over the transom'** American slang for the arrival of unsolicited mss.

**PB** Abbreviation for 'paperback', a book whose covers are made of paper, card or laminated card.

**Photo-journalism** Journalism in which the text is of secondary importance to the photographs.

**Photo-story script** A story told in the form of a sequence of photographs with captions.

**Picture agency** An organisation which keeps photographs and/or illustrations in store and leases reproduction rights to writers and publishers.

**Picture fees** 1. Fees paid by an author or publisher for the right to reproduce illustrations in which he does not hold the copyright. 2. Fees paid by a publisher to an author or journalist for the right to reproduce his illustrations.

**Picture-story script** A story told in a sequence of artist-drawn pictures, with dialogue shown in balloons, and perhaps with supplementary captions.

**Plagiarism** The use, whether deliberate or accidental, of work in which the copyright is held by someone else.

**Plot** The storyline, the central thread with which everything else that happens is interwoven.

**PLR** Public Lending Right. A system of monetary reward for writers, based on the number of times their works are borrowed from public libraries. The award any one writer will receive depends on the book meeting certain conditions and being borrowed a minimum number of times. *See also* the section on **Other relevant organisations**.

**Professional journal** A publication produced specifically for circulation in a particular profession, for example *The Lancet* (medicine).

**Proofs** An impression or series of impressions of the typeset matter for checking and correction before the final printing.

**Proposal** A suggested idea for a book, usually put to the publisher in the form of an initial query ('Would you be interested in...?'), then as a synopsis of the whole work, with a sample chapter or two.

**Publisher's reader** A person employed by a publisher to evaluate a manuscript and to give the publisher a written summary and report, to help the publisher to assess its potential as a published work.

**Readership** A collective term applied to the people who habitually read a particular publication.

**Reading fee** A fee charged by an agent, magazine or publisher to read a submitted ms. Usually refundable in the event of acceptance and publication.

**Rights** Those parts of an author's copyright which he leases to a publisher, as specified in a contract.

**Royalty** A percentage of the published price of a book payable to the author under the terms of his contract. How much he receives depends on the percentage agreed and on the number of copies sold.

**SAE (US SASE)** Stamped addressed envelope (US self-addressed stamped envelope). An envelope addressed back to the sender, and bearing adequate postage stamps.

**'Scissors-and-paste job'** A contemptuous term applied to work that consists of material 'lifted' from reference books, encyclopedias, magazines and so on, rearranged, and then passed off as an original piece of writing.

**Screenplay** A film-script that includes cinematic information — for example, camera movements — as well as dialogue.

**'Slush-pile'** A term applied to the unsolicited mss which accumulate in an editorial office. So-called because of the sentimental and emotional content of a large proportion of these mss.

**Small presses** Small businesses, often one-person operations, producing publications ranging from duplicated pamphlets to bound books, and of very variable production quality. Seldom profitable, and usually financed by their proprietors and/or other enthusiasts.

**Staff-writer** (US **staffer**) A writer employed and salaried by a publisher, as distinct from a freelance.

**Storyline** The sequence of events that keeps the action of a plot moving forward: 'and then...and then...and next...'

**Strap/strapline** An identification line at the top of a manuscript page.

**Submission** A manuscript that is sent — submitted — to a publisher, with a view to possible publication.

**Subsidiary rights** A term usually applied to rights other than UK book publication rights. For example, film and TV rights, foreign language rights, serial rights and so on.

**Synopsis** A précis or condensed version of the theme and contents of a book, giving a clear outline and breakdown of the proposed text.

**Syntax** The way in which words or phrases are put together.

**Taboos** Subjects, words, references and so on that are not acceptable to certain publications.

**Technical writing** The writing of company and product manuals, reports, engineering and computing manuals and so on.

**Text** The body of typeset matter in a book, as distinct from headings, footnotes, illustrations and so on.

**Textbooks** A term usually applied to books written for the educational market.

**Theme** The subject of a story, the thread that links the narrative, for example a moral concept — 'crime doesn't pay', 'love conquers all' — or a specific human quality, like courage or greed, self-sacrifice or failure. Not to be confused with the plot.

**Trade journal** A publication produced for circulation among practitioners and companies in a particular trade or industry, for example *The Bookseller, The Grocer.*

**Unsolicited manuscript/unsolicited submission** A piece of work sent to a publisher completely without invitation.

**Usual terms/usual rates** The usual rate of payment which a publication offers to freelance writers.

**'Vanity' publishing** A term applied to the publication of work on behalf of an author who pays someone else to publish the work for him.

**Voucher copy** A copy of a single issue of a publication, sent free to a writer whose work appears in that issue, as evidence (to vouch) that the work has in fact been published.

**Word processor (wp)** A machine which uses computer logic to accept, store and retrieve material for editing and eventual printing out in typewritten or printed form.

**Workshop** A group of people meeting to exchange opinions and constructive suggestions on current work, usually under the guidance of a writer/tutor.

**Writers' circle** A group of people meeting to read, discuss and possibly criticise each other's work. Differs from a workshop in that the work is usually done at home before instead of during the meeting.

**Writers' seminar** A meeting of writers, usually lasting at least one day, where there are guest speakers, discussions, possibly workshops, and where writers can make contact with other writers, both published and unpublished.

**Yearbook** A book published annually, reviewing the past year's events and/or updating information.

# Associations and Societies Open to Unpublished Writers

**Association of Comics Enthusiasts (ACE).** Founded for collectors of British comics and strips, this is a good source of information about current comics and strip cartoons. ACE issues *Comic Cuts Newsletter,* factsheets on comic-related topics (including publishers), a monthly Comic Chronology feature (includes current and new comics). Membership fee is £5, which covers all the above and more. Contact Denis Gifford, 80 Silverdale, Sydenham, London SE26 4SJ (Tel: (01) 699 7725).

**Association of Little Presses (ALP).** New members always welcome. Formed to bring together, inform and assist small presses (these are usually one- or two-person outfits) publishing poetry and other literature. Issues a (roughly) bi-monthly newsletter of information about the world of little presses, giving printing and production tips, sources of stationery supplies, services and so on, *Poetry and Little Press Information* magazine (PALPI), and the current catalogue of *Little Press Books in Print.* Annual subscription £7.50, which covers all the above. Contact Bob Cobbing, ALP, 89A Petherton Road, London N5 2QT (Tel: (01) 226 2657).

**Blind Authors' Association.** Formed to help blind or partially sighted writers. There's a library of material helpful to writers, and two quarterly programmes:
1. A review of news and information, advice from successful writers, requests for help from members and so on.
2. Stories, poems and articles submitted by members for criticism by the membership.

All this is on tape. Members supply their own blank tapes to receive the recorded material. A comprehensive writing course is also available on tape (current cost about £95). Membership fee £3 per annum. Contact Editor/Organiser John May, 'Brierdene', Croit e Quill Road, Lonan, Isle of Man (Tel: (0624) 781 349). No SAE required here — UK stamps are not valid in the Isle of Man.

**British Academy of Songwriters, Composers & Authors (BASCA).** (*Note:* 'Authors' in this title refers to authors of lyrics.) Associate membership is available to unpublished songwriters. BASCA offers a comprehensive professional advice and guidance service. Members receive a quarterly information magazine, *BASCA News*. Associate Membership fee £11.50 per annum. For full details of BASCA's services, contact General Secretary Marilyn Worsley, BASCA, 148 Charing Cross Road, London WC2H 0LB (Tel: (01) 240 2823/4).

**British Amateur Press Association.** Brings together people interested in the various arts and crafts of journalism *as a hobby*. Issues *The British Amateur Journalist*. Members also receive a bi-monthly 'bundle' — a news bulletin plus a selection of members' privately produced magazines. Membership fee £4 (reduced rates for families). Contact the Treasurer, Mr Laurence E. Linford, 78 Tennyson Road, Stretford, London E15 4DR (Tel: (01) 555 2052).

**The British Fantasy Society (BFS).** Covers the fantasy, horror and science fiction fields. Publishes a regular newsletter of information and reviews, covering books, films and events, and its own magazine *Dark Horizons*, which contains fiction and articles, and also several other magazines of specialist interest in this field. Organises an annual fantasy conference, 'Fantasycon', and the British Fantasy Awards. Membership open to all. All the BFS magazines are included in the annual subscription fee, UK £8, USA $18, Canada $19, Europe £10, elsewhere £15 (sterling, US or Canadian currency only). Contact Secretary Di Wathen, 15 Stanley Road, Morden, Surrey SM4 5DE.

**British Science Fiction Association.** Publishes a critical journal, *Vector,* a review supplement, *Paperback Inferno*, and a newsletter, *Matrix*, all bi-monthly. *Focus* (three a year) has articles on writing and markets, to encourage amateur and new writers. There's a postal workshop, *Orbiter*, for beginning writers, and a science fiction information service. For more details and current membership fees, contact Paul Kincaid, 114 Guildhall Street, Folkestone, Kent CT20 1ES.

**Bureau of Freelance Photographers (BFP).** Membership open to professional and amateur photographers and writers. Offers a monthly, *BFP Market Newsletter*, full of factual, verified information on current markets for photographs and photo-journalism, an advisory service for freelance photographers, a fee recovery service, and discounts on photographic goods and services. Publishes an annual 250 page *BFP Freelance Photographers' Market Handbook*. All the above are included in the annual membership fee of £25. For more details (including a free two-month introductory offer) contact the editor, John Tracy, Bureau of Freelance Photographers, Focus House, 497 Green Lanes, London N13 4BP (Tel: (01) 882 3315).

**Comedy Writers Association.** A non-profit-making club to help new comedy writers sell their work. Aims to help and encourage fellow writers, to provide members with regular market information, and to promote comedy writing. Offers a bi-monthly newsletter, monthly market information, meetings in various parts of the country (members are encouraged to contact each other), visits to radio and TV studios, rehearsals and programme recordings, a library geared to comedy writing, and an annual working holiday/conference. CWA members work at professional levels, and if you haven't already sold material to radio and/or TV you'll be asked to complete a set of test exercises which will be assessed by the committee. For further details and current membership fee, contact the President, Ken Rock, 61 Parry Road, Ashmore Park, Wolverhampton, West Midlands WV11 2PS (Tel: (0902) 722729).

**The J. T. Edson Appreciation Society.** Formed to bring J. T. and his readers together — 'he is a writer who cares'. The society issues a bi-monthly newsletter, discussing J. T.'s books and their characters and answering members' questions about the Old West. There are jokes and puzzles, competitions and a pen-pals section. J. T. Edson takes an active part in the society, and it's informal and friendly. They hope to organise an annual get-together. *Please note:* Neither J. T. nor the society can undertake criticism, so don't send mss. Subscription is about £4. Contact the Secretary, Mrs Joan Coulter, J. T. Edson Appreciation Society, PO Box 13, Melton Mowbray, Leics.

**Fellowship of Christian Writers.** Membership open 'to those who desire to serve Jesus Christ in the realm of writing.' Concentrates mainly on imaginative writing — novels (especially children's) and poetry — but welcomes those interested in factual writing. Subscription covers a quarterly news-sheet of advice and news about Christian writing and writers, and a monthly writers' workshop held in Forest Gate, London. Organises Writers' Days (members £5.50, visitors £8), mss criticism (£5 for first 1,000 words, then £3 per thousand, maximum 10,000). No poetry criticism. Subscription £5. Contact Hon. Secretary Joan Gordon-Farleigh, 8 Harold Road, Deal CT14 6QJ (Tel: (0304) 360982).

**The Friends of the Arvon Foundation.** Active in support of the Arvon Foundation. Issues a regular newsletter of information about events, competitions, writers' markets and literature, and details of current and projected Arvon writers' courses. Keeps you in contact with events and with other writers. Membership fee £5. Contact Hon. Secretary Edna Eglinton, 9 North Street, North Tawton, Devon EX20 2DE (Tel: (083) 782 816).

**London Screenwriters Workshop.** Open to anyone interested in writing for film and TV, and to those working in these and related media. Practical workshops held in London, and out-of-town members can send in scripts for reading and criticism by practising screenwriters. Has members throughout the UK and beyond. Issues a newsletter, and advises members about agents and producers. Annual subscription £12. Contact London Screenwriters Workshop, 78 Grove House, Chelsea Manor Street, London SW3 5QB (Tel: (0923) 31342 — enquiries only).

**London Writer Circle.** Open to London and country members. Details from the Enrolment Secretary, Mrs A. Miller, 28 Knowsley Road, London SW11 5BL.

**National Poetry Foundation.** Offers a bi-annual magazine, *Pause*, appraisal of your poems, possible publication in *Pause*, possible eventual publication of a booklet of your poems (at no cost to you), news of competitions and literature, all covered by the annual membership fee of £12. Contact the Founder, Johnathon Clifford, 27 Mill Road, Fareham, Hants PO16 0TH (Tel: (0329) 822218).

**New Playwrights Trust.** Open to all playwrights and others interested in the development of playwriting. Offers comprehensive information services and a script-reading service. 1988–9 membership costs £5 (unwaged £2.50, groups £10). The fees will probably increase slightly in 1989–90. For more details contact New Playwrights Trust, Whitechapel Library, 77 Whitechapel High Street, London E1 7QX (Tel: (01) 377 5429).

**The Penman Club.** World-wide membership open to all writers. Subscription covers *all* the following: free criticism of mss, free advice on any writing/publishing problems, free library service (you only pay postage), pen friendships, free ten-lesson literary course. Registration fee £3, plus annual subscription, one year £5.25, three years £15, five years £20. Contact the General Secretary, Leonard G. Stubbs FRSA, 175 Pall Mall, Leigh-on-Sea, Essex SS9 1RE (Tel: (0702) 74438).

**Players and Playwrights.** Meets in London on most Monday evenings.

A long-established society of amateur and professional writers and actors who write, read and perform plays. No specific prerequisites for membership. Fees are £5 per annum plus £1 per session. Contact Hon. Secretary B. J. Rogers, 56 The Drive, Beckenham, Kent BR3 1EQ (Tel: (01) 658 3813).

**The Poetry Book Society.** A book club. Subscription covers a quarterly bulletin, a free annual poetry anthology, and the opportunity to buy quality poetry books at discount prices. New members get a £4 book voucher. Subscription £17.50. Contact The Poetry Book Society, 21 Earls Court Square, London SW5 9DE (Tel: (01) 244 9792).

**The Poetry Society.** Membership open to all. Fee covers a year's subscription to *Poetry Review Quarterly* and members' information bulletin, advance notification of all Poetry Society events, entitlement to reduced admission charges/concessionary tickets to Literature Festival Council events, access to special offers from the Poetry Society Bookshop, reduced rates for use of the Critical Service (see section on **Services**). Fees: London £15, elsewhere in Britain/Ireland £12, Europe £13, outside Europe £13 surface mail, £23 airmail. Life membership £250. Contact The Poetry Society, 21 Earls Court Square, London SW5 9DE (Tel: (01) 373 2551). *Note:* although the Poetry Society and The Poetry Book Society share an address, they are separate organisations, and should be addressed separately.

**The Romantic Novelists' Association.** Offers Probationary Membership to unpublished romantic novelists, conditional on being prepared to submit a full length ms to be considered for the Netta Muskett Award for New Writers. The entry fee is £20, which must be paid on joining, and which is not returnable. For details of membership, conditions and how to submit your ms, contact the Treasurer, Mrs Marina Oliver, 'Half Hidden', West Lane, Bledlow, Nr Princes Risborough, Bucks HP17 9PF (Tel: (08444) 5973).

**The Scottish Association of Writers.** Groups, clubs and workshops for writers throughout Scotland. Organises conferences, competitions and weekend schools for members. Membership open to any group of writers (no minimum number of members) forming a club/circle/workshop. Individual postal membership can be arranged. Fees £5 per club plus £1 fee per member. Details from the Secretary, Mrs Beth Thomson, 1D Vicarland Place, Kirkhill, Cambuslang, Glasgow G72 8QE (Tel: (041) 641 7203).

**Society of International Songwriters & Composers (SISC).** Aims to give advice and guidance to its songwriter, composer and home recordist members. Open to amateur as well as professional songwriters. Offers members song assessments, collaboration between lyric writers and composers, information on music publishers' requirements, advice about copyright, contracts, demonstration tapes, presentation and so on. A free quarterly magazine, *Songwriting and Composing*, is issued to members. Fee £12 per annum. Contact the Chairman, Roderick G. Jones, 12 Trewartha Road, Praa Sands, Penzance, Cornwall TR20 9ST (Tel: (0736) 762 826). SISC has an associated music publishing company, First Time Music (Publishing) UK Ltd, at the same address.

**The University of the Third Age (U3A).** Membership open to retired people of all ages (no academic qualifications required). Has branches throughout the country. Organises all kinds of educational, creative and leisure activities — many branches include creative writing groups. For names and addresses of local branches and contacts, write to Dianne Norton, Executive Secretary, The Third Age Trust, National U3A Office, 6 Parkside Gardens, London SW19 5EY (Tel: (01) 947 0401). Please send 6″ x 10″ SAE.

# Services

## CRITICISM AND MANUSCRIPT ASSESSMENT SERVICES

**The London School of Journalism** undertakes the criticism and editing of full-length novels, memoirs, biographies and other literary works. Three forms of criticism are offered:
1. A general report and opinion.
2. A more detailed and constructive criticism with suggested revision.
3. Complete editing of a manuscript.
The fees will depend on which service you choose. Details from The Secretary, The London School of Journalism, 19 Hertford Street, Park Lane, London W1X 8BB (Tel: (01) 499 8250).

**National Poetry Foundation** will give appraisals of your poems as part of the benefits of membership, which costs £12 per annum. Contact the Founder, Johnathon Clifford, National Poetry Foundation, 27 Mill Road, Fareham, Hants PO16 0TH (Tel: (0320) 822218).

**Oriel Critical Service for Writers** (for writers living in Wales only). This service is supported by the Welsh Arts Council. It offers constructive advice based on a close reading of submitted work, and gives rigorous and detailed criticism. The fee for each sample of work is £5 — a sample should not exceed 200 lines of poetry or 3,000 words of prose. A report of about 1,000 words will be given, in complete confidence. For full details of the service, and how to submit your ms for criticism, contact Oriel Critical Service, Oriel Bookshop, 53 Charles Street, Cardiff CF1 4ED (Tel: (0222) 395548).

**The Penman Criticism Service.** Membership of the Penman Club entitles you to criticism of all mss at no further charge. *See* **Associations and Societies Open to Unpublished Writers** on page 152.

**The Poetry Society Critical Service.** Founded by Norman Hidden. Professional experts provide detailed reports on poetry mss. The fee per work unit of up to 200 lines (one unit per submission) is £23 including VAT (Poetry Society members £17.25, quoting membership number). A report of two to four pages is given in confidence after up to ten weeks. With the report and your returned ms you'll get four free information sheets. If you're not sure that your work is ready for submission to rigorous criticism, you can obtain an annotated book list of suggested preparatory reading on request with an SAE. For an application form or book list, contact The Administrator, Poetry Society Critical Service, 21 Earls Court Square, London SW5 9DE (Tel: (01) 373 7861 and 2551).

**Radio and Television Script Criticism Service:** Rosemary Horstmann offers expert criticism and tuition — see Chapter 12. Contact Rosemary Horstmann, 43 Westcombe Park Road, Blackheath, London SE3 7QZ (Tel: (01) 853 4706).

**Scriptmate Readers-for-Writers Advisory Service:** A personal service on almost every field of writing, offered in two related stages:
1.  A reader's report with constructive revision suggestions, sent to you direct from a professional reader selected specifically for you.
2.  Re-assessment after revision, with advice on where and how to submit your ms to publishers or literary agents.

The Scriptmate Professional Advisory Team includes Harold Brooks-Baker, Ann Kritzinger, John Pawsey and Douglas Sutherland.

Scriptmate is *not* a writing-school or a literary agency. The Stage One fee is about £100, Stage Two by arrangement, depending on the length and type of ms involved. For full details and current charges, and also details of other Scriptmate services, contact Ann Kritzinger, Scriptmate, 11 Rosemont Road, London NW3 6NG (Tel: (01) 341 7650).

## INFORMATION SERVICES AND SOURCES

**The Association of Free Newspapers (AFN)** publishes the annual *A–Z of Britain's Free Newspapers and Magazines*, a directory of the names, addresses, distribution areas and circulation figures of the country's thousands of 'freebies'. It costs about £30, but is distributed free to advertising agencies and national advertisers. For details of current price and availability, contact The Publisher, Sarah Barnes, AFN, Ladybellegate House, Longsmith Street, Gloucester GL1 2HT (Tel: (0452) 308100).

**Bookfinding service:** Geoff and Karinda FitzGerald, proprietors of Jubilee Books, will search the world for the book you want, with no search fee and no postal charges — you pay only for the book. Contact Jubilee Books, 203B Locking Road, Weston-super-Mare, Avon BS23 3HG (Tel: (0934) 33166).

**Book Trust:** A marvellous source of information on all things literary, prizes, publications, exhibitions, readings and so on. **Book Information Services** will deal with your enquiries, either by letter or by telephone — there's a special direct line: (01) 874 8526. They'll send you details of all their services in return for an SAE ($6\frac{1}{2}''$ x 9″). Contact the Publicity Officer, Book Trust, Book House, 45 East Hill, London SW18 2QZ (Tel: (01) 870 9055/8).

**British Library Newspaper Library**, Colindale Avenue, London NW9 5HE (Tel: (01) 636 1544).

**Freelance Press Services** are agents for Writer's Digest Books, USA, and for *Writer's Digest* and *The Writer* magazines (both American). They'll send a book catalogue on request. They also publish *Freelance Market News*, a monthly bulletin of market information for writers, and organise occasional writers' seminars. For full details of their services, contact Managing Editor Arthur Waite, Freelance Press Services, 5/9 Bexley Square, Salford, Manchester M3 6DB (Tel: (061) 832 5079).

**French's Theatre Bookshop (Samuel French Ltd)** is an excellent source of books and cassettes on all the media and performing arts, including writing. They'll send you lists on request, and it helps if you specify your particular area or areas of interest. French's operate a comprehensive mail order service. Details from French's Theatre Bookshop, 52 Fitzroy Street, London W1P 6JR (Tel: (01) 387 9373).

**Greeting Card and Calendar Association** is a professional association of greeting card companies. Where possible they will try to help with individual enquiries about their members' requirements. Contact the Information Officer, Greeting Card and Calendar Association, 6 Wimpole Street, London W1M 8AS (Tel: (01) 637 7692).

The Association's bi-monthly magazine, *Greetings*, is available to anyone who wants to subscribe to it. It's an ideal source of information about current greeting card and calendar production, new companies and so on. The subscription is £6 per annum. Contact Haymarket Publishing, 38–42 Hampton Road, Teddington, Middlesex TW11 0JE (Tel: (01) 977 8787).

**Literary research service:** All subjects, but specialising in biography, and police and criminal history (including associated political and social effects). Other literary services, including 'ghosting' are available. Contact Rod Richards, 'Tracking Line', 23 Spearhill, Lichfield, Staffs WS14 9UD (Tel: (0543) 254748).

**Network Scotland Ltd**, an information broker delivering high quality information on a broad range of subjects. A leaflet detailing services can be obtained on request. For general information, contact Network Scotland Ltd, 74 Victoria Crescent Road, Glasgow G12 9JQ (Tel: (041) 357 1774). For information about education and training services, contact Joan Rees, Senior Information Officer, Network Scotland Ltd, Education and Training Section, Unit 11a, Anderston Cross Centre, Glasgow G2 7PH (Tel: (041) 225 5859).

**NIACE (The National Institute of Adult Continuing Education, England and Wales)** publish (twice a year) the booklet *Residential Short Courses*, £1.30 post paid. Contact Anne Blandamer, Directory Editor, NIACE, 19B De Montfort Street, Leicester LE1 7GE (Tel: (0533) 551451).

**Oriel, The Welsh Arts Council's Bookshop**, offers a variety of services to writers and small and new publishers; as well as the Writers' Critical Service for writers living in Wales, there's a regular programme of literary events, an *ad hoc* advice service to small and new publishers looking for ways to market their publications, a regularly updated address list of small presses and little magazines, and a mail order service selling books about books and writing. Details of all Oriel's services and their book lists from Peter Finch, Oriel Bookshop, 53 Charles Street, Cardiff CF1 4ED (Tel: (0222) 395548).

**Photographic agency:** Popperfoto, Paul Popper Limited, 24 Bride Lane, Fleet Street, London EC4Y 8DR (Tel: (01) 353 9665/6).

**Press Cuttings Service:** Facts and information for article writers. Contact Mrs Pat Kenderdine, 'Redlands', Carlton Road, Carlton Miniott, Thirsk, North Yorkshire YO7 4LX (Tel: (0845) 24163).

## LITERARY AGENTS

**Diane Burston, Literary Agent,** 46 Cromwell Avenue, Highgate, London N6 5HL (Tel: (01) 340 6130).

**Dorian Literary Agency (Dorothy Lumley)**, 'Suncrest', 35 Longcroft Avenue, Brixham, Devon TQ5 0DS (Tel: (08045) 59390).

**The Jane Gregory Agency** and **Gregory and Radice, Literary Agents,** are both at the same address: 4 Westwick Gardens, London W14 0BU (Tel: (01) 603 5168).

**The Penman Literary Agency** is one of the services offered by The

Penman Club — *see* **Associations and Societies Open to Unpublished Writers** on page 152.

## PRINTING/PUBLISHING SERVICES

**Afton Press** print your own poetry and prose on greeting cards to order. Contact Penny Glenday, The Afton Press (Freepost), 18 Ireland Street, Carnoustie, Scotland DD7 6XA (Tel: (0241) 55415).

**Deanhouse Limited, Publishers and Print Originators** (academic material only). Contact Roland P. Seymour, Deanhouse Limited, The Mews House, Court Walk, Betley, Near Crewe, Cheshire CW3 9DP (Tel: (0270) 820053).

**Scriptmate,** editorial services and short-run laser-printed paperbacks. Scriptmate offers a range of services which are worth looking at in detail. For more information contact Ann Kritzinger, Scriptmate, 11 Rosemont Road, London NW3 6NG (Tel: (01) 341 7650).

## WRITERS' ACCOMMODATION SERVICE

**The London Writing Rooms,** Farringdon House, 105–107 Farringdon Road, Clerkenwell, London EC1R 3BT (Tel: (01) 278 7879). Rooms available for writers to rent as places of work.

# Writing Courses

## CORRESPONDENCE AND DEGREE COURSES

**The Academy of Children's Writers Ltd,** 3 Regal Lane, Soham, Ely, Cambridgeshire CB7 5BA (Tel: (0353) 721899).

**Children's Authorship.** Course, details from Children's Features, Freelance Press Services, 5/9 Bexley Square, Salford, Manchester M3 6DB (Tel: (061) 832 5079).

**Eston Limited,** Training Division, Norman House, Heritage Gate, Friargate, Derby DE1 1DD (Tel: (0332) 360202). (Technical writing only.)

**London School of Journalism,** 19 Hertford Street, Park Lane, London W1Y 8BB (Tel: (01) 499 8250).

**Penman Postal Courses.** Free to members of The Penman Club. Details from General Secretary Leonard G. Stubbs FRSA, 175 Pall Mall, Leigh-on-Sea, Essex SS9 1RE (Tel: (0702) 74438).

**Tutortex Services,** 55 Lightburn Avenue, Ulverston, Cumbria LA12 0DL (Tel: (0229) 56333). (Technical writing only.)

**University of East Anglia.** MA in Creative Writing. A postgraduate full-time course. Details from the Graduate Admissions Secretary, Aileen Davies, School of English and American Studies, University of East Anglia, Norwich NR4 7TJ (Tel: (0603) 56161).

**University of Essex.** MA in Women Writing. Details from the Graduate Secretary, Dorothy Gibson, Department of Literature, University of Essex, Wivenhoe Park, Colchester, Essex CO4 3SQ (Tel: (0206) 873333).

**University of Lancaster.** MA in Creative Writing (not for beginners). Details from Dr David Craig, B124 Lonsdale College, University of Lancaster, Bailrigg, Lancaster LA1 4YN (Tel: (0524) 65201, extension 318).

**The Writing School,** 18–20 High Road, Wood Green, London N22 6BX (Tel: (01) 888 1242).

## SEMINARS AND RESIDENTIAL COURSES

**The Arvon Foundation** runs residential courses at two centres in England: Lumb Bank, Heptonstall, Hebden Bridge, West Yorkshire, HX7 6DF (Tel: (070 681) 6582), and Totleigh Barton, Sheepwash, Devon EX21 5NS.

**London Media Workshops** run seminars (between one and five days) on writing for radio, TV, video and the Press. Contact Mrs Sylvia Angel, London Media Workshops, 101 King's Drive, Gravesend, Kent DA12 5BQ (Tel: (0474) 64676).

**Swanwick Writers' Summer School**, an annual six-day course held in August. Usually very heavily oversubscribed, so book early. Contact the Secretary, Mrs Philippa Boland, The Red House, Marden Hill, Crowborough, Sussex TN6 1XN. (*Note:* Swanwick is in Derbyshire.)

# More Useful Addresses

## PROFESSIONAL ASSOCIATIONS

The Arts Council of Great Britain, 105 Piccadilly, London W1V 0AU (Tel: (01) 629 9495).

British Broadcasting Corporation (BBC), Broadcasting House, Portland Place, London W1A 1AA (Tel: (01) 580 4468).

National Council for the Training of Journalists (NCTJ), Carlton House, Hemnall, Epping, Essex CM16 4NL (Tel: (0378) 72395).

National Union of Journalists (NUJ), Acorn House, 314 Gray's Inn Road, London WC1X 8DP (Tel: (01) 278 7916).

The Newspaper Society Training Department, Whitefriars House, Carmelite Street, London EC4Y 0BL (Tel: (01) 583 3311).

The Society of Authors, 84 Drayton Gardens, London SW10 9SB (Tel: (01) 373 6642).

The Writers' Guild of Great Britain, 430 Edgware Road, London W2 1EH (Tel: (01) 723 8074).

## PUBLISHERS MENTIONED IN THE TEXT

W. H. Allen & Co. PLC, 44 Hill Street, London W1X 8LB (Tel: (01) 493 6777).

Allison & Busby, 44 Hill Street, London W1X 8LB (Tel: (01) 493 6777).

Andersen Press Ltd, 62–65 Chandos Place, London WC2N 4NW (Tel: (01) 240 8162).

Argus Books Ltd, 1 Golden Square, London W1R 3BB (Tel: (01) 437 0626).

Bantam Press, 61-63 Uxbridge Road, London W5 5SA (Tel: (01) 579 2652).

BBC Books, 35 Marylebone High Street, London W1M 4AA (Tel: (01) 743 5588).

B. T. Batsford Ltd, 4 Fitzhardinge Street, London W1 0AH (Tel: (01) 486 8484).

A. & C. Black (Publishers) Ltd, 35 Bedford Row, London WC1R 4JH (Tel: (01) 242 0946).

Blackie Children's Books, 7 Leicester Place, London WC2H 7BP (Tel: (01) 734 7521).

Basil Blackwell Ltd, 108 Cowley Road, Oxford OX4 1JF (Tel: (0865) 722146).

Blandford Publishing Ltd, Link House, 25 West Street, Poole, Dorset BH15 2SS (Tel: (0202) 671171).

Blueprint Publishing Ltd, The Finsbury Business Centre, 40 Bowling Green Lane, London EC1R 0NE (Tel: (01) 278 0333).

The Bodley Head Ltd, 32 Bedford Square, London WC1B 3EL (Tel: (01) 631 4434).

Brimax Books Ltd, 4–5 Studlands Park Industrial Estate, Exning Road, Newmarket, Suffolk CB8 7AU (Tel: (0638) 664611).

Buchan & Enright Publishers Ltd, 45 The Broadway, Tolworth, Surrey KT6 7DW (Tel: (01) 390 7768).

Cambridge University Press, The Edinburgh Building, Shaftesbury Road, Cambridge CB2 2RU (Tel: (0223) 312393).

Jonathan Cape Ltd, 32 Bedford Square, London WC1B 3EL (Tel: (01) 636 3344.

Cassell PLC, Artillery House, Artillery Row, London SW1P 1RT (Tel: (01) 222 7676).

Century Hutchinson Ltd, 62–65 Chandos Place, London WC2N 4NW (Tel: (01) 240 3411).

Collins Publishers, 8 Grafton Street, London W1X 3LA (Tel: (01) 493 7070).

Constable & Co. Ltd, 10 Orange Street, London WC2H 7EG (Tel: (01) 930 0801–7).

Coronet — an imprint of Hodder & Stoughton Ltd.

Darton, Longman & Todd, 89 Lillie Road, London SW6 1UD (Tel: (01) 385 2341).

David & Charles Publishers PLC, Brunel House, Forde Road, Newton Abbot, Devon TQ12 4PU (Tel: (0626) 61121).

J. M. Dent & Sons Ltd, 33 Welbeck Street, London W1M 8LX. (Tel: (01) 486 7233).

André Deutsch Ltd, 105–106 Great Russell Street, London WC1B 3LJ (Tel: (01) 580 2746).

Richard Drew Publishing Limited, 6 Clairmont Gardens, Glasgow G3 7LW (Tel: (041) 333 9341).

Ebury Press, 27–37 Broadwick Street, London W1V 1FR (Tel: (01) 439 7144).

Elm Tree Books (Hamish Hamilton Ltd), 27 Wrights Lane, London W8 5TZ (Tel: (01) 938 3388).

Exley Publications Ltd, 16 Chalk Hill, Watford, Herts WD1 4BN (Tel: (0923) 50505).

Faber & Faber Ltd, 3 Queen Square, London WC1N 3AU (Tel: (01) 278 6881).

Samuel French Ltd, 52 Fitzroy Street, London W1P 6JR (Tel: (01) 387 9373). (Plays only.)

Victor Gollancz Ltd, 14 Henrietta Street, London WC2E 8QJ (Tel: (01) 836 2006).

Grafton Books Ltd, 8 Grafton Street, London W1X 3LA (Tel: (01) 493 7070).

Robert Hale Ltd, Clerkenwell House, 45–47 Clerkenwell Green, London EC1R 0HT (Tel: (01) 251 2661).

Hamish Hamilton Ltd, 27 Wrights Lane, London W8 5TZ (Tel: (01) 938 3388).

Harrap Ltd, 19–23 Ludgate Hill, London EC4M 7PD (Tel: (01) 248 6444).

Headline Book Publishing PLC, Headline House, 79 Great Titchfield Street, London W1P 7FN (Tel: (01) 631 1687).

William Heinemann Ltd, Michelin House, 81 Fulham Road, London SW3 6RB (Tel: (01) 581 9393).

Hodder & Stoughton Ltd, 47 Bedford Square, London WC1B 3DP (Tel: (01) 636 9851).

InterChange Books, 15 Wilkin Street, London NW5 3NG (Tel: (01) 267 9421).

Michael Joseph Ltd, 27 Wrights Lane, London W8 5TZ (Tel: (01) 937 7255).

Kogan Page Ltd, 120 Pentonville Road, London N1 9JN (Tel: (01) 278 0433).

Charles Letts & Co. Ltd, Diary House, Borough Road, London SE1 1DW (Tel: (01) 407 8891).

Lion Publishing PLC, Icknield Way, Tring, Herts HP23 4LE (Tel: (044 282) 5151).

Longman Group UK Ltd, Longman House, Burnt Mill, Harlow, Essex CM20 2JE (Tel: (0279) 26721).

Macdonald & Co. Ltd, 3rd Floor, Greater London House, Hampstead Road, London NW1 7QX (Tel: (01) 377 4600).

Macmillan Publishers Ltd, 4 Little Essex Street, London WC2R 3LF (Tel: (01) 836 6633).

Malvern Publishing Co. Ltd, 32 Old Street, Upton-upon-Severn, Worcestershire WR8 0HW (Tel: (06846) 4408).

Methuen & Co. Ltd, Michelin House, 81 Fulham Road, London SW3 6RB (Tel: (01) 581 9393).

Mills & Boon Ltd, Eaton House, 18–24 Paradise Road, Richmond, Surrey TW9 1SR (Tel: (01) 948 0444). Mills & Boon Reader Service, for cassette and guidelines: PO Box 236, Thornton Road, Croydon, Surrey CR9 3RU (Tel: (01) 684 2141).

Mitchell Beazley Ltd, Artists House, 14/15 Manette Street, London W1V 5LB (Tel: (01) 439 7211).

Mulholland-Wirral, The Croft, School Avenue, Little Neston, South Wirral L64 4BS. (Telephone unlisted.)

New English Library, Mill Road, Dunton Green, Sevenoaks, Kent TN13 2YA (Tel: (0732) 450111).

Northcote House Publishers Ltd, Harper & Row House, Estover Road, Plymouth PL6 7PZ (Tel: (0752) 705251).

Octopus Books Ltd, Michelin House, 81 Fulham Road, London SW3 6RB (Tel: (01) 581 9393).

Oxford University Press, Walton Street, Oxford OX2 6DP (Tel: (0865) 56767).

Pan Books Ltd, 18–21 Cavaye Place, London SW10 9PG (Tel: (01) 373 6070).

Pandora Press, 11 New Fetter Lane, London EC4P 4EE (Tel: (01) 583 9855).

Pelham Books Ltd, 27 Wrights Lane, London W8 5TZ (Tel: (01) 937 7255).

Pelican — an imprint of Penguin Books Ltd.

Penguin Books Ltd, 27 Wrights Lane, London W8 5TZ (Tel: (01) 938 2200).

Judy Piatkus (Publishers) Ltd, 5 Windmill Street, London W1P 1HF (Tel: (01) 631 0710).

Poplar Press Ltd. Enquiries about Poplar Press books and catalogues should now be sent to David & Charles Publishers PLC.

Puffin Plus Books — an imprint of Penguin Books Ltd.

SCM Press Ltd, 26–30 Tottenham Road, London N1 4BZ (Tel: (01) 249 7262).

Severn House Publishers, 2nd Floor, 40–42 William IV Street, London WC2N 4DF (Tel: (01) 240 9683).

Simon & Schuster Ltd, West Garden Place, Kendal Street, London W2 2AQ (Tel: (01) 724 7577).

SPCK (Society for Promoting Christian Knowledge), Holy Trinity Church, Marylebone Road, London NW1 4DU (Tel: (01) 387 5282).

Sphere Books Ltd, 27 Wrights Lane, London W8 5TZ (Tel: (01) 937 8070).

D. C. Thomson & Co. Ltd, Albert Square, Dundee, Scotland DD1 9QJ (Tel: (0382) 23131).

Thorsons Publishing Group Ltd, Denington Estate, Wellingborough, Northants NN8 2RQ (Tel: (0933) 76031).

Unwin Hyman Ltd, Denmark House, 37–39 Queen Elizabeth Street, London SE1 3QB (Tel: (01) 407 0709).

Viking/Viking Kestrel, 27 Wrights Lane, London W8 5TZ (Tel: (01) 938 2200).

Virago Press Ltd, Centro House, 20–23 Mandela Street, Camden Town, London NW1 0HQ (Tel: (01) 383 5150).

Walker Books, 87 Vauxhall Walk, London SE11 5HJ (Tel: (01) 793 0909).

J. Whitaker & Sons Ltd, 12 Dyott Street, London WC1A 1DF (Tel: (01) 836 8911).

The Women's Press, 34 Great Sutton Street, London EC1V 0DX (Tel: (01) 251 3007).

Writer's Digest Books, 9933 Alliance Road, Cincinnati, Ohio 45242, USA.

## THEATRE COMPANIES

Liverpool Playhouse, Williamson Square, Liverpool L1 1EL (Tel: (051) 709 8478).

Paines Plough, 'The Writers Company', 121–122 Tottenham Court Road, London W1P 9HN (Tel: (01) 380 1188).

The Traverse Theatre, 112 West Bow, Grassmarket, Edinburgh EH1 2PD (Tel: (031) 226 2633).

## OTHER RELEVANT ORGANISATIONS

- **Aslib, The Association for Information Management,** Information House, 26–27 Boswell Street, London WC1N 3JZ (Tel: (01) 430 2671).

- **The Association of Authors' Agents,** 11 Jubilee Place, London SW3 3TE (Tel: (01) 352 4311 and 2182).

- **British Library Copyright Receipt Office,** 2 Sheraton Street, London W1V 4BH (Tel: (01) 636 1544).

- **British Theatre Association.** Access to the Association's Play Library, the most comprehensive in the world, is free and open to anyone who visits the premises. Membership (subscription from £15 per annum) gives you access to the reference and lending sections of the library. Address: The Darwin Infill Building, Regents College, Inner Circle, Regents Park, London NW1 4NS (Tel: (01) 935 2571).

- **Cartoonists Club of Great Britain,** Secretary Mike Turner, 11 Simons Lane, Colchester, Essex (Tel: (0206) 67283).

- **Catholic Writers Guild,** 1 Leopold Road, London W5 3PB (Tel: (01) 992 3954).

- **Crime Writers' Association.** Membership open only to *published* writers of crime fiction or serious works on crime. Associate membership available to publishers, journalists and booksellers specialising in crime literature. Members frequently speak at writers' seminars, so look out for these. Address: PO Box 172, Tring, Herts HP23 5LP.

- **Institute of Contemporary Arts.** Among its activities and services, the Institute produces a series of videotapes, 'Writers in Conversation'. Prices start at £75 per video, with reductions for quantity purchases. The authors on tape include P. D. James, Brian Aldiss, Joseph Heller, Harold Pinter, Fay Weldon and dozens of others. Details from Fenella Greenfield, Director of Video, Institute of Contemporary Arts, The Mall, London SW1Y 5AH (Tel: (01) 930 0493).

- **Public Lending Right Office,** Bayheath House, Prince Regent Street, Stockton-on-Tees, Cleveland TS18 1DF (Tel: (0642) 604699). All authors who get a book published should register it immediately for PLR.

- **Scottish Arts Council,** 19 Charlotte Square, Edinburgh EH2 4DF (Tel: (031) 226 6051).

- **Society of Civil Service Authors,** Secretary Mrs J. M. Hykin, 38 The Highway, Sutton, Surrey SM2 5QT. (To encourage authorship by past and present members of the Civil Service.)

- **Society of Women Writers and Journalists (SWWJ).** For published writers. You can join on a probationary basis when you've had just a little work published. Contact the Hon. Secretary, Mrs Olive McDonald, 2 St Lawrence Close, Edgware, Middlesex HA8 6RB.

- **Theatre Writers' Union,** Actors Centre, 4 Chenies Street, London WC1E 7EP (Tel: (01) 631 3619). For all writers working in the theatre.

- **Welsh Arts Council,** Holst House, Museum Place, Cardiff CF1 3NX (Tel: (0222) 394711).

- **Welsh Books Council (Cyngor Llyfrau Cymraeg),** Castell Brychan, Aberystwyth, Dyfed SY23 2JB (Tel: (0970) 4151/3). Encourages interest in Welsh literature, and supports writers of books in the Welsh language.

# Further Reading

## BOOKS FOR WRITERS

Joan Aiken, *The Way to Write for Children* (Elm Tree, 1982), pb £6.95.
William Ash, *The Way to Write Radio Drama* (Elm Tree, 1986), pb £6.95.
Brad Ashton, *How to Write Comedy* (Elm Tree, 1983), pb £6.95.
Donna Baker, *How to Write Stories for Magazines* (Allison & Busby 1986), pb £2.95.
Jill Baker, *Copy Prep* (Blueprint, 1987), hb £14.95.
Michael Baldwin, *The Way to Write Poetry* (Elm Tree, 1983), pb £6.95.
Michael Baldwin, *The Way to Write Short Stories* (Elm Tree, 1986), pb £6.95.
Michael Barnard, *Magazine and Journal Production* (Blueprint, 1986), hb £19.95.
Julian Birkett, *Word Power — A Guide to Creative Writing* (A. & C. Black, 1983), pb £5.95.
*Blackwell Guide for Authors* (Basil Blackwell, 1985), pb £2.95.
Anthony Blond, *The Book Book* (Jonathan Cape, 1985), hb £9.95.
Paul Darcy Boles, *Story Crafting* (David & Charles, 1987), hb £9.95.
David Bolt, *An Author's Handbook* (Piatkus, 1986), pb £3.95.
John Braine, *Writing a Novel* (Methuen, 1974), pb £5.95.
Dorothea Brande, *Becoming a Writer* (Papermac, first published 1934), pb £3.95.
William Brohaugh, *Professional Etiquette for Writers* (Writer's Digest Books, 1986), hb $9.95.*
Stephen Citron, *Songwriting* (Hodder & Stoughton, 1987), hb £14.95.
Lisa Collier Cool, *How to Sell Every Magazine Article You Write* (Writer's Digest Books, 1986), hb $14.95.*
Bruce M. Cooper, *Writing Technical Reports* (Pelican, 1964), pb £2.95.
Alastair Crompton, *The Craft of Copywriting* (Century Hutchinson, 1987), pb £6.95.
Alastair Crompton, *Do Your Own Advertising* (Century Hutchinson, 1987), pb £6.95.
Sheila Davis, *The Craft of Lyric Writing* (Writer's Digest Books, 1986), hb $18.95.*

Christopher Derrick, *Reader's Report* (Gollancz, 1970). Out of print, but your library might have a copy.

Dianne Doubtfire, *The Craft of Novel-Writing* (Allison & Busby, 1978), pb £2.95.

Dianne Doubtfire, *Teach Yourself Creative Writing* (Hodder & Stoughton 'Teach Yourself' Books, 1983), pb £2.95.

Christopher Evans, *Writing Science Fiction* (A. & C. Black, 1988), pb £4.95.

Hilary Evans, *The Art of Picture Research* (David & Charles, 1979), hb £12.50 (£13.50 post paid from Mary Evans Picture Library, 1 Tranquil Vale, Blackheath, London SE3 0BU (Tel: (01) 318 0034).

John Fairfax and John Moat, *The Way to Write* (Elm Tree, 1981), pb £6.95.

Peter Finch, *How to Publish Your Poetry* (Allison & Busby, 1985), pb £3.95.

Peter Finch, *How to Publish Yourself* (Allison & Busby, 1988), pb £3.95.

J. A. Fletcher & D. F. Gowing, *The Business Guide to Effective Writing* (Kogan Page, revised ed. 1987), pb £6.95.

Tom Gallacher, *The Way to Write for the Stage* (Elm Tree, 1988), pb £6.95.

William Gentz and Lee Roddy, *Writing to Inspire* (Writer's Digest Books, 1986), pb $14.95.*

Fay Goldie, *How to Write Stories and Novels that Sell* (Malvern, 1986), pb £3.95.

Fay Goldie, *Successful Freelance Journalism* (Oxford University Press, 1984), pb £4.95.

Ray Hammond, *The Writer and the Word Processor* (Coronet, 1987), pb £3.95.

Brendan Hennessy, *Essential Feature Writing* (Heinemann Professional Publishing, 1988) hb £12.95.

Patricia Highsmith, *Plotting and Writing Suspense Fiction* (Poplar Press, 1983), pb £4.95.

John Hines, *The Way to Write Magazine Articles* (Elm Tree, 1987), pb £6.95.

Rosemary Horstmann, *Writing for Radio* (A. & C. Black, 1988), pb £5.95.

Raymond Hull, *How to Write 'How-To' Books and Articles* (Writer's Digest Books, 1981), pb $8.95.*

André Jute, *Writing a Thriller* (A. & C. Black, 1986), pb £4.95.

H. R. F. Keating, *Writing Crime Fiction* (A. & C. Black, 1986), pb £4.95.

Paul Kerton, *The Freelance Writer's Handbook* (Ebury Press, 1986), pb £5.95.

Paddy Kitchen, *The Way to Write Novels* (Elm Tree, 1983), pb £6.95.

Michael Legat, *An Author's Guide to Publishing* (Robert Hale, 1982), pb £4.95.

Michael Legat, *Writing for Pleasure and Profit* (Robert Hale, 1986), pb £4.95.

Claudia Lewis, *Writing for Young Children* (Poplar Press, revised edn. 1984), pb £4.95.

Ian Linton, *Writing for a Living* (Kogan Page, 2nd edn. 1988), pb £5.95.

Yvonne MacManus, *You Can Write a Romance and Get it Published!* (Severn House, 1983), hb £5.95.

Rhona Martin, *Writing Historical Fiction* (A. & C. Black, 1988), pb £4.95.

Alan McKenzie, *How to Draw and Sell Comic Strips* (Macdonald Orbis, 1988), hb £12.95.

Peter Medina, *Careers in Journalism* (Kogan Page, 3rd edn. 1988), pb £3.95.

William Miller, *Screenwriting for Narrative Film and Television* (Harrap Columbus, 1988), pb £7.95.

Harry Mulholland, *Guide to Self-Publishing — The A-Z of Getting Yourself into Print* (Mulholland-Wirral, 1984), pb £5.95 from bookshops, or £6.70 post-paid from the publisher.

Eric Paice, *The Way to Write for Television* (Elm Tree, 1987), pb £6.95.

Dan Poynter & Mindy Bingham, *Is there a book inside you?* (Exley, 1986), pb £6.95.

Gary Provost, *Make Every Word Count* (Writer's Digest Books, 1980), pb $7.95.*

Philip Davies Roberts, *How Poetry Works* (Pelican, 1986), pb £3.95.

Geoffrey Rogers, *Editing for Print* (Macdonald, 1986), hb £9.95.

Larry Sandman (ed.), *A Guide to Greeting Card Writing* (Writer's Digest Books, 1980), pb $8.95.*

Jean Saunders, *The Craft of Writing Romance* (Allison & Busby, 1986), pb £2.95.

Jean Saunders, *Writing Step by Step* (Allison & Busby, 1988), hb £9.95.

Keith Smith, *Marketing for Small Publishers* (InterChange Books, 1980), pb £4.50.

Evelyn A. Stenbock, *Teach Yourself to Write* (Writer's Digest Books, 1982), pb $9.95.*

Ian Stewart, *The Business Writing Workbook* (Kogan Page, 1987), pb £4.95.

Julian Symons, *Bloody Murder* (Penguin, revised edn. 1985), pb £3.95.

Liz Taylor, *The Writing Business* (Severn House, 1985), pb £3.95.

Felicity Trotman, *How to Write and Illustrate Children's Books* (Macdonald Orbis, 1988), hb £12.95.

Gordon Wells, *The Craft of Writing Articles* (Allison & Busby, 1983), pb £3.95.

Gordon Wells, *The Magazine Writer's Handbook* (Allison & Busby, 2nd edn. 1987), pb £3.95.

Gordon Wells, *Writers' Questions Answered* (Allison & Busby, 1986), pb £3.95.

John Whale, *Put it in Writing* (Dent, 1984), pb £2.95.

Phyllis Whitney, *Guide to Fiction Writing* (Poplar Press, 1984), pb £4.95.

Mary Wibberley, *To Writers With Love* (Buchan & Enright, 2nd edn. 1987), pb £4.95.

*Writing for the BBC* (BBC Publications), pb £3.95.

Jonathan Zeitlyn, *Print — how you can do it yourself* (InterChange Books, revised edn. 1986), pb £3.95.

*The prices of the American Writer's Digest Books listed are given in US dollars, to give you an idea of their cost — the UK price varies with the exchange rate. These books are stocked or can be ordered by some of the larger city booksellers, or you can order them from Freelance Press Services or from Poplar Press, both of whom will send current catalogues on request. The address in America is: Writer's Digest Books, 9933 Alliance Road, Cincinnati, Ohio 45242, USA.

## MAGAZINES AND NEWSPAPERS MENTIONED IN THE TEXT

*Annabel, The Beezer, Blue Jeans, Dundee Sporting Post, Jackie, My Weekly, People's Friend, Secrets,* and *Victor* are all published by D. C. Thomson & Co. Ltd, Albert Square, Dundee DD1 9QJ (Tel: (0382) 23131).

*Bella*, Shirley House, 25–27 Camden Road, London NW1 9LL (Tel: (01) 284 0909).

*Best*, Portland House, Stag Place, London SW1E 5AU (Tel: (01) 245 8847).

*British Judo*, 16 Upper Woburn Place, London WC1H 0QH (Tel: (01) 387 9304).

*Canal and Riverboat*, Stanley House, 9 West Street, Epsom, Surrey KT18 7RL (Tel: (03727) 41411).

*Caring for Handicaps*, Stanley House, 9 West Street, Epsom, Surrey KT18 7RL (Tel: (03727) 41411).

*The Catholic Herald*, Herald House, Lambs Passage, Bunhill Row, London EC1Y 8TQ (Tel: (01) 588 3101/5).

*Christian Family*, 37 Elm Road, New Malden, Surrey KT3 3HB (Tel: (01) 942 9761).

*Christian Herald*, Herald House, Dominion Road, Worthing, West Sussex BN14 8IP (Tel: (0903) 821082).

*Christian Woman*, Herald House, Dominion Road, Worthing, West Sussex BN14 8IP (Tel: (0903) 821082).

*Church Times*, 7 Portugal Street, London WC2A 2HP (Tel: (01) 405 0844).

*Darts World*, World Magazines Ltd, 2 Park Lane, Croydon, Surrey CR9 1HA (Tel: (01) 681 2837).

*Ellery Queen's Mystery Magazine*, Davis Publications Inc., 380 Lexington Avenue, New York NY 10017.

*Home and Country*, 39 Eccleston Street, London SW1W 9NT (Tel: (01) 730 0307).

*Jewish Chronicle*, 25 Furnival Street, London EC4A 1JT (Tel: (01) 405 9252).

*Jewish Telegraph*, Telegraph House, 11 Park Hill, Bury Old Road, Prestwich, Manchester M25 8HH (Tel: (061) 740 9321).

*Practical Photography*, Bushfield House, Orton Centre, Peterborough OE2 0UW (Tel: (0733) 237111).

*Private Eye*, 6 Carlisle Street, London W1V 5RG (Tel: (01) 437 4017).

*Punch*, 23–27 Tudor Street, London EC4Y 0HR (Tel: (01) 583 9199).

*The Stage and Television Today,* Stage House, 47 Bermondsey Street, London Bridge, London SE1 3XT (Tel: (01) 403 1818).

*The Tablet,* 48 Great Peter Street, London SW1P 2HB (Tel: (01) 222 7462).

*Weekend*, New Carmelite House, London EC4Y 0JA (Tel: (01) 353 6000).

*Woman*, King's Reach Tower, Stamford Street, London SE1 9LS (Tel: (01) 261 5413).

*Woman's Own*, King's Reach Tower, Stamford Street, London SE1 9LS (Tel: (01) 261 5474).

*Woman's Weekly*, King's Reach Tower, Stamford Street, London SE1 9LS (Tel: (01) 261 6131).

## PUBLICATIONS OF PARTICULAR INTEREST TO NEW WRITERS

*Acumen* magazine, editor Patricia Oxley. Published April and October. Single copy £2. Current subscription rates, UK and overseas, sent on request. Address: 6 The Mount, Higher Furzeham, Brixham, South Devon TQ5 8QY, England.

*The Author*, editor Derek Parker. The official magazine of the Society of Authors. Quarterly. Available to non-members on subscription: £10 per annum. Address: Publications Department, The Society of Authors,

84 Drayton Gardens, London SW10 9SB (Tel: (01) 373 6642).

*Book and Magazine Collector*, editor John Dean. Monthly. Available from newsagents at £1.50 or direct from the publishers by subscription, UK £21, Eire £29 (Irish), Europe £25 (all up rate) or £22 (reduced rate), USA $50, Canada $65, Australia $75. Rates to other countries on request. Address: The Magazine Editor, Book and Magazine Collector, 43/45 St Mary's Road, Ealing, London W5 5RQ, England (Tel: (01) 579 1082).

*The Bookseller*, 'the organ of the book trade', editor Louis Baum. Weekly magazine, price 95p (special Spring Books and Autumn Books issues about £7.50) from newsagents or on subscription: UK £57, overseas £70 (air mail extra). Address: 12 Dyott Street, London WC1A 1DF (Tel: (01) 836 8911).

*Envoi* (poetry only), editor Anne Lewis-Smith. Three issues a year. Subscription UK £6, overseas $11.50 (air mail $14.00). Back copies £1, single current copy £2. Address: Pen Ffordd, Newport, Dyfed, Wales SA42 0QT.

*First Time* (poetry only), editor Josephine Austin. Two issues a year. Subscription £2.50, back copies 50 pence. Address: Burdett Cottage, 4 Burdett Place, George Street, Old Town, Hastings, East Sussex TN34 3ED.

*Freelance Market News* (formerly *Contributors Bulletin*), editor Mrs Saundrea Williams. Monthly (except August). Subscription (which includes a quarterly 'overseas markets' supplement) UK £17.50 for 11 issues, £9.75 for six issues, overseas (air mailed) £21 for 11 issues. Address: Freelance Press Services, 5/9 Bexley Square, Salford, Manchester M3 6DB (Tel: (061) 832 5079).

*Freelance Writing and Photography*, editor Charlotte Everest-Phillips. Quarterly magazine for writers and photo-journalists. Subscription £7.50 per annum. Address: Victoria House, Victoria Road, Hale, Cheshire WA15 2BP (Tel: (061) 928 5588).

*Interzone* (science fiction and fantasy), editors Simon Ounsley and Brian Pringle. Quarterly. Subscription UK £7.50 (cheques and postal orders crossed and made payable to Interzone), overseas £8.50, payable by International Money Order. USA subscriptions may be paid by US dollar check, $13 sea mail, $16 air mail. Lifetime subscriptions UK

£100, overseas $200 or equivalent ($250 air mail). Back issues UK £1.95, overseas £2.50 (US $4 sea mail, $5 air mail). All issues in print except number 5. Address: 124 Osborne Road, Brighton BN1 6LU, Sussex, England (Tel: (0273) 504710).

*Outposts Poetry Quarterly*, editor Roland John. Subscription UK £8 per annum, £15 for two years, USA £18 per annum. Single copy UK £2.50, USA $6. Address: 26 Cedar Road, Sutton, Surrey SM2 5DG (Tel: (01) 643 1970).

*Panurge*, editor David Almond. Two issues a year. Subscription UK £3.50 (single copy £2), overseas £4.50 (£7 air mail). Address: 22 Belle Grove West, Spital Tongues, Newcastle upon Tyne NE2 4LT, England (Tel: (091) 232 7669).

*Prospice*, editors J. C. R. Green and Roger Elkin. Quarterly. Subscription UK £12.50, US $25, elsewhere payable preferably in sterling, otherwise at the US dollar rate converted to local currency. Air mail rates, add 100%. Sample copies UK £2.50, overseas US$5 or equivalent *in bills* (to help with exchange charges) or $10 or equivalent by cheque. Subscription and sample prices include a free copy of comprehensive writers' guidelines if requested. The guideline booklet can be ordered separately at £1.95 (UK). Address: Aquila Publishing (UK) Limited, PO Box 418, Leek, Staffordshire, ST13 8UX, England (Tel: (0538) 387368).

*Proteus* fantasy adventure game magazine, editor Mike Kenward, is published by Wimborne Publishing Limited, 6 Church Street, Wimborne, Dorset BH21 1JH (Tel: (0202) 881749).

*Publishing News*, editor Fred Newman. Weekly. 80p from newsagents (tell your supplier it's distributed by Spotlight). The editor will send you a copy direct for £1. Address: 43 Museum Street, London WC1A 1LY (Tel: (01) 404 0304).

*Stand Magazine*, editors Jon Silkin and Lorna Tracy. Quarterly. Subscription UK £7.60 per annum, overseas £8.40 (air mail by arrangement). Sample copy £2. Address: 179 Wingrove Road, Newcastle upon Tyne NE4 9DA, England (Tel: (091) 273 3280).

*Success* (writers' magazine), editor Kate Dean. Bi-monthly. Subscription UK £10 (6 issues), £5.50 (3 issues). EC residents who don't have sterling bank accounts are requested to pay by Eurocheque (in sterling). USA/Canada residents may send dollar bills instead of cheques. Cheques/postal orders should be crossed and made payable to Success. UK residents can get a sample copy in return for two second class stamps. Address: 17 Andrews Crescent, Peterborough PE4 6XL, England.

*The Wordsmith* (for writers using word processors/computers), editor David Hewson. Bi-monthly. Subscription UK £10, single issue £2 (UK only). Current overseas rates on request. Address: Mandarin Publishing, The Old House, Church Road, Kennington, Ashford, Kent TN24 9DQ, England (Tel: (0233) 39776).

*Writer's Monthly* (writers' magazine), editor Alison Gibbs. Subscription about £30 per annum (the publishers wouldn't supply any information on projected rates or plans). They frequently offer a free copy — watch for the adverts in the national press, usually on the literary pages. Address: 18–20 High Road, London N22 6BX (Tel: (01) 888 1242).

*The Writers' Newsletter*, editor Patrick Campbell. The official organ of The Writers' Guild of Great Britain. Ten issues a year. Available to non-members on subscription, £7 per annum. Address: The Writers' Guild of Great Britain, 430 Edgware Road, London W2 1EH (Tel: (01) 723 8074).

*Writers' Own Magazine* (writers' magazine), editor Mrs Eileen M. Pickering. Quarterly. Subscription UK £4 per annum, overseas £6 per annum. Single copy £1 (overseas £1.50). Address: 121 Highbury Grove, Clapham, Bedford MK41 6DU (Tel: (0234) 65982).

*The Writers' Rostrum* (writers' magazine), editor Jenny Chaplin. Quarterly. Subscription UK £5 per annum. Overseas rates on application. Address: 14 Ardbeg Road, Rothesay, Bute PA20 0NJ, Scotland.

*Writing* (writers' magazine), editor Barbara Horsfall. Three issues a year. Subscription UK £3 per annum (single copy £1.25), USA $10.50 (single copy $4), elsewhere £4.50 per annum (single copy £1.60), all post paid. Special rates available for creative writing/poetry groups. Please send SAE for details. Address: 87 Brookhouse Road, Farnborough, Hants GU14 0BU, England.

### Cassette
*'And then he kissed her...'*. £4.95 post paid from Mills & Boon Ltd, Reader Service, PO Box 236, Thornton Road, Croydon, Surrey CR9

3HU (Tel: (01) 684 2141).

## RECOMMENDED REFERENCE BOOKS

*Chambers Twentieth Century Dictionary* (4th ed. 1983), hb £13.95.
*Dictionary of Literary Terms*, Martin Gray (Longman York Handbooks 1984), pb £2.95.
*Guide to English Usage* (Longman, 1988), hb £10.95.
*The Oxford Dictionary for Writers and Editors* (Clarendon/OUP, 1981), hb £8.95.
*Pears Cyclopedia* (Pelham Books, annual), hb £10.95.
*Penguin Dictionary of Historical Slang*, ed. Eric Partridge (Penguin 1972), pb £7.95.
*Pocket Dictionary of Publishing Terms*, Henry Jacob (Macdonald, 1976), pb £1.50.
*The Reader's Encyclopedia* (A.& C. Black, 1987), hb £19.95.
*Research for Writers*, Ann Hoffmann (A. & C. Black, 1986), pb £6.95.
*Roget's Thesaurus* (Longman 1982), hb £11.50; (Collins pb ed. £3.50).
*Spell Well*, compiled by Kirkpatrick and Schwartz (Chambers, 1980), hb £2.95.
*Type It Yourself*, Brenda Rowe (Penguin, 1975), pb £2.95.
*Whitaker's Almanack* (J. Whitaker, annual), hb £15.95; pb £7.50.
*Willing's Press Guide* (IPC Business Press, annual), hb about £50.
*The Writers' & Artists' Yearbook* (A. & C. Black, annual), pb £5.95.
*The Writer's Handbook* (Macmillan, annual), pb £5.95.
*Writer's Market* (USA) (Writer's Digest Books, annual) hb $22.

**Consult these in the library**
*British Books in Print* (J. Whitaker).
*Cassell's Media Directory.*

## USEFUL BOOKLETS

*All Write Now* by Pat Saunders. Journalism for disabled people. 50p plus 20p postage from RADAR (The Royal Association for Disability and Rehabilitation), 25 Mortimer Street, London W1N 8AB (Tel: (01) 637 5400).

*Author's Guide.* Free on receipt of a first class stamp, from David & Charles Publishers PLC, Brunel House, Newton Abbot, Devon TQ12 4PU (Tel: (0626) 61121).

*BBC Television Market Information for Writers.* Free from the

Television Script Unit, BBC Television Centre, Wood Lane, London W12 7RJ.

*Directory of Writers' Circles.* £3 post-paid from Jill Dick, 'Oldacre', Horderns Park Road, Chapel-en-le-Frith, Derbyshire SK12 6SY. (Please make cheques payable to Laurence Pollinger Ltd.)

*First Heard* (broadcast poetry). £1.25 post-paid (cheques/postal orders payable to 'Children in Need') from Peggy Poole, 'First Heard', BBC Radio Merseyside, 55 Paradise Street, Liverpool L1 3EP (Tel: (051) 708 5500).

*Guidelines for Educational Writers* and *Sell your Writing.* £1.50 each post-paid from the Society of Authors, 84 Drayton Gardens, London SW10 9SB (Tel: (01) 373 6642).

*Howard MBE* is a collection of the late Howard Sergeant's poems, writings and thoughts on poetry and poetry writing, edited by his widow, Jean. It costs £4.80 post paid from the National Poetry Foundation, 27 Mill Road, Fareham, Hants PO16 0TH.

*The Making of a Newspaper.* 40p from the Newspaper Society, Training Dept, Whitefriars House, Carmelite Street, London EC4Y 0BL (Tel: (01) 583 3311).

*Notes on Radio Drama.* Free from the Script Editor (Radio Drama), BBC, Broadcasting House, London W1A 1AA.

*The Playscript from Scratch.* £2.25 post-paid from David Huxley, Haslemere Publications, 16 Haslemere Drive, Cheadle Hulme, Cheadle, Cheshire SK8 6JY (Tel: (061) 485 7484).

*Publishing Your Own Book — A Guide for Authors and Societies*, by H. L. Gray. £1.20 post paid from Deanhouse Ltd, The Mews House, Court Walk, Betley, Near Crewe, Cheshire CW3 9DP (Tel: (0270) 820053).

*Theatre Writing Schemes* (brochure) on request from the Drama Director, The Arts Council of Great Britain, 105 Piccadilly, London W1V 0AU.

# Index